# DAD
# YOU SUCK

ALSO BY TIM DOWLING

*How To Be a Husband*

# DAD
# YOU SUCK

## Tim Dowling

4th ESTATE • *London*

4th Estate
An imprint of HarperCollins*Publishers*
1 London Bridge Street
London SE1 9GF
www.4thEstate.co.uk

First published in Great Britain in 2017 by 4th Estate

1

Printed and bound in Great Britain by
Clays Ltd, St Ives plc

**MIX**
Paper from
responsible sources
**FSC® C007454**

FSC is a non-profit international organisation established to promote the responsible management of the world's forests. Products carrying the FSC label are independently certified to assure consumers that they come from forests that are managed to meet the social, economic and ecological needs of present and future generations, and other controlled sources.

Find out more about HarperCollins and the environment at
www.harpercollins.co.uk/green

*To my sons, Barnaby, Johnnie and Will
– if you're reading this, call me.*

# CONTENTS

# INTRODUCTION

I am sitting at a boardroom table in the offices of a PR company, interviewing an ex-*Apprentice* contestant called Raef. Though he was booted off the show in week nine, after Alan Sugar dismissed him as 'a lot of hot air', Raef remains possessed of an unshakeable self-belief. I find this irritating, and I have to keep reminding myself that it's not Raef's fault he believes in himself. It's probably something to do with the way he was raised.

Raef is in the middle of a digressive burst of false modesty, which, I think to myself, is probably the only kind of modesty he has ever known. As he speaks I flip through my reporter's notepad, looking for a question I may have scribbled down earlier and forgotten about, a question searching and incisive enough to pierce Raef's shiny carapace of confidence. Instead, I find a page on which one of my children has written 'DAD YOU SUCK' in large block capitals, using a marker pen.

When I get home an hour later, there is a new Personal Power newsletter in my email inbox. I've been receiving these regular motivational updates from an internet life coach ever since I signed up for an online course while writing a newspaper feature about life coaching. This was months ago, but I don't know how to make the emails stop. These days I rarely read beyond the subject line, which usually says something like, 'Hi Tim – Self-Confidence Is A Magic Key' or, 'Hi Tim – Happiness Is All Around You If You Look'.

This latest newsletter is headed, 'Hi Tim – How Would It Feel If You Knew Why You Were Here?' and goes on to detail a prolonged exercise in soul-searching that is supposed to end with you receiving a short, secret phrase that sums up your reason for being on earth. I think about my life's true purpose for a bit, but I can't come up with a secret phrase better than 'DAD YOU SUCK'.

That evening my wife comes home from her bookshop and immediately launches into a tireless inventory of my failings. This has become a weekly event, which coincides with the shop's late opening – my wife has spent many hours being polite to people, and she has already said all the nice things she is going to say today. I get whatever's left. My oldest son knows it's Thursday again, and he has come down to watch.

'You didn't slice the bread,' she says, peering into the bread bin.

'The slicing machine was broken,' I lie. I have developed a dread of the bread slicer at the supermarket, the repeated operation of which only serves to underscore the grinding futility of existence. Also, it strikes me as vaguely unhygienic.

'No, it wasn't,' my wife says, turning to the child. 'Your father is hopeless.'

At this point it dawns on me that it is my wife's life purpose to drain my self-esteem at every opportunity. Instantly, I feel lighter. My shoulders drop back, as if I were spreading invisible wings. My wife seems to notice the change. She is staring at me intently.

'Your hair's looking a bit thin at the front,' she says. She turns to the boy. 'Your father is losing his hair, I'm afraid.'

'I'm married,' I say. 'I no longer need hair.'

'He has to say that because he's going bald.'

'She's just trying to flatten my self-esteem,' I tell the boy. 'She can't help it. It's her life's purpose.'

'She's like a self-esteem roller,' he says.

'That's very good,' I say. 'I can use that.'

My wife glares at both of us.

'No, you cannot use it,' she says. 'I'm not allowing it. You cannot write that I am like a self-esteem roller.'

'Yes I can,' I say. 'I can use it if I want.' I look at the boy. 'Can't I?' He thinks for a minute.

'Five pounds,' he says finally.

'Done,' I say.


People occasionally ask me if I find writing about my children in a weekly newspaper column ethically challenging. The truth is, I never really thought about it until people started asking, and by then it was too late to stop. I had never intended to write about my children – the column was always meant to be about me – but I soon found that it was almost impossible to keep them out of the narrative, because they talk all the time. They interject, they interrupt, they ask impertinent and largely irrelevant questions, and they repeat stupid things I've said in what they think is an amusing approximation of my voice.

A domestic scene from which all childish input has been artificially excised, for reasons of privacy or ethics or being a good father or whatever, immediately loses its claim to veracity. Consider this brief dialogue between a husband and wife:

> Wife: You're having supper with your family. Are you ever going to say anything?
> Husband: No. Can someone pass the salad?
> Wife: Oh my God. I can't live like this.

All very kitchen sink, but I think you'll agree something is missing. Now read it again, with the omitted dialogue restored:

> Wife: You're at supper with your family. Are you ever going to say anything?
> Youngest child: Can I get down?
> Husband: No. Can someone pass the salad?
> Middle child: You're the salad.
> Wife: Oh my God. I can't live like this.

As the above scene illustrates, the real problem with writing about children is not a question of privacy, but one of passivity. The writer is meant to be a neutral observer of existence, a position not exactly compatible with father-hood, which is generally considered a more hands-on business. My wife thinks I should do more about my children's mealtime behaviour than find it column-worthy.

I accept that writing about children has its grey areas. Perhaps, in assuming the role of narrator, I am altering my relationship with my sons in ways I don't understand. It's conceivable that by writing about my family I am experiencing fatherhood at one remove, like someone who films his life on his phone. It could be that instead of prioritizing my children's happiness, I am simply prioritizing my version of events.

Like anyone else, children have a right to ownership of their lives and may object to being traduced in print on a weekly basis, although in my experience it's rarely a problem that £5 won't fix. By a longstanding tradition begun on that evening when my wife came home from her bookshop, that is the fee payable to my children when I quote them directly, although it is their obligation to spot the quotation and claim the money. Since this would require them to read my column on a regular basis, it means that in practice I hardly ever have to shell out.

For me the hardest task of fatherhood was always the oppressive obligation to lead by example. Nothing worries me more than the possibility that my sons are using me as some kind of role model. As it is they've been present on countless occasions when I have, as we say in my homeland, completely lost my shit. During these stressful moments I have often wished to turn to them as a judge might to a jury and say, 'Please strike the next few minutes from the record', but then, within the week, I will have committed my less than exemplary behaviour to print. Indeed, many of those instances are chronicled in the pages ahead. It's not because I'm any less ashamed now; it's because if I left them out there wouldn't be enough for a book.

Perhaps this is my life's true purpose: maybe I'm here to teach my sons that self-esteem comes and goes – it can get rolled right out of you at short notice – but that you still can get by in life without any, as long as you don't want to be a contestant on *The Apprentice*. That, at least, is my experience. And for what it's worth, my example.

TD

# CHAPTER ONE

Whenever I hear the term 'co-parenting', I think back to those long-ago early mornings when my wife and I would try to lever each other off the edge of the bed, in the tacit understanding that the first person to hit the floor would be obliged to go and tend a crying infant. You couldn't call it teamwork, exactly, but since we were both equally determined not to be the one to get up, it was broadly fair. Later I came to realize that the only real help one parent can give another is an offer to take the child – or the children – a considerable distance away for an agreed period of time.

'Have fun,' my wife would say, shutting the door on us. 'Don't come back early.'

I should really use a separate word to signify the kind of parenting I do when my wife isn't around to share in the joy of it. For lack of a better term, let's call it 'fathering'. These intervals tend to differ in tone and style from co-parenting, and often end with me listing things we needn't tell Mum about. I don't mean for it to undermine the parenting best practice we've agreed upon as a couple, but I won't pretend that fathering isn't characterized by a certain drift from established methods. I just do whatever works, even after it stops working.

On a typical Saturday I find myself at a loose end in London with my three children and my friend Mark, who is visiting from America. My wife, meanwhile, is working in her bookshop all day. We have already dropped by for a visit, and we have already been asked to leave. I've made no further plans.

Our options are subsequently curtailed by rain. The children are hungry. Hungry children can be cranky and short-tempered, but in my experience they are also listless and biddable, and this is how I like it. If you keep promising them food, they will keep walking. They might complain, but they lack the energy for real rebellion. So I am strolling through the pouring rain with three slope-shouldered boys moaning and dragging their heels behind me. This, I think, is about as good as it gets.

Eventually, when I feel we've used up enough afternoon, we stop at a noodle bar for a late lunch. The children spot iced tea on the menu. To them, iced tea is an exotic American treat, like powdered pink lemonade or bubblegum-flavoured jellybeans. To me, an American, it is tea with some ice in it that costs £4, but I find myself in the mood to reward their patience. The food arrives, spirits lift and we all chat volubly. A strange sense of fatherly competence begins to steal over me. Only later in life will I come to recognize this feeling as a bad omen.

There is a lull after the plates have been cleared when the waiter seems to forget all about us. I'm trying to carry on a conversation with Mark, but the younger two, their blood sugar levels restored, have begun to poke each other with chopsticks as part of a game that is rapidly getting out of hand. I threaten to separate them. When they continue I carry out my threat, deftly sliding them apart and sitting down on the bench between them. As soon as I resume the conversation, they start poking each other behind my back. Then they start poking me. When I turn to remonstrate with the youngest one, the oldest leans across the table and sticks the point of a chopstick in my ear. This, I decide, is a step too far.

I accept that there must be something inherently amusing about my sense of humour deserting me. I don't know why this is. No one laughs when my wife has a sense-of-humour failure, sometimes not for the rest of the week. But the children are hysterical, giggling maniacally and poking me over and over again with chopsticks, in the ribs, in the arms, in the side of my head. I am hissing for them to stop, and doing my most threatening eyebrows.

More than once I try to restore order by saying, 'OK, I'm serious now' but this only makes them laugh louder and poke harder. If I'm quick enough I can snatch a chopstick away – after a few minutes I have a big handful – but this is a noodle bar; there are lots of chopsticks lying around. At one point the youngest child actually goes to the counter to ask for more.

Before long I have completely lost control of the situation. Everywhere I look I catch the eye of someone staring at me with either pity or scorn, or some sieved mixture of the two. None of them is our waiter. My debit card has been sitting on the little dish for fifteen minutes, and still he hasn't appeared.

I look at Mark, who is also looking at me with pity and scorn, and clearly wishing he was doing it from farther away. I shrug my shoulders at him wearily, and then recoil as the point of a chopstick stabs into my neck.

'It's because you gave them iced tea,' he says.

When you have young children in London, most weekends break down into a basic binary choice: Science Museum or dinosaurs. Because the Science Museum is right next to the Natural History Museum, it's an argument that can continue for your entire journey there. The choice never mattered to me, because I came to hate both places more or less equally. Once a PR person offered me the chance to spend the whole night in the Science Museum with my children and a bunch of other kids and parents. It sounded like some kind of community punishment order. I've never done anything wrong enough to deserve that.

There is, of course, a wealth of culture on offer in London, much of it child-friendly. Over years of weekends I enthusiastically made the case for many enticing alternatives: plays, galleries, street parties, food festivals, exhibitions, one-off happenings. And every time I did, my three children would look at me blankly. Then two would say 'Science Museum' and one would say 'dinosaurs'.

Eventually I learned to lie about where we were going.

'This is boring,' says the youngest one, slumping against a temporary fence. He has a point. My three sons and I have made a trip to see the Serpentine Pavilion in Kensington Gardens, the majority of us under protest. The temporary pavilion – they put up a new one every spring – architecturally intriguing though it may be from the outside, is presently closed for some private event. Through its glass walls we can see someone giving what appears to be a lecture to a seated audience. I tell the youngest one he's lucky, that it would probably be even more boring if we were inside.

'Can we get an ice cream now?' he says. As I look round for the nearest ice cream van I spy a poster for the adjacent Serpentine Gallery, which is currently exhibiting recent work by the US artist Jeff Koons. I had been planning to see it anyway, but I don't imagine I'll be back this way on my own any time soon.

'Let's go in there first,' I say. 'Just for a bit.'

The Serpentine Gallery has always been, to my mind, an easy-going cultural venue. As well as being a showcase for new and sometimes challenging art, it's also free and in a park, and consequently full of sticky toddlers at weekends. They know their audience, and are correspondingly accommodating. But today things are different: gallery staff are holding people at the entrance in order to deliver a stern warning about the fragility of the artwork on display. My children chat all the way through it. Once inside we gather round a sculpture consisting of a large inflatable cartoon caterpillar poking through the rungs of a folding stepladder, and stare.

'I'm really not impressed by this,' says the middle one. 'What's so great about a pool toy stuck in a ladder?' I explain that with this sculpture, as with much of the work of Jeff Koons, all is not as it seems.

'It may look like an ordinary blow-up toy,' I say, 'but it's actually made of metal.' I begin to doubt these words even as they leave my mouth. I must have read this fact somewhere, but the caterpillar before me looks exactly like an inflatable toy, with perfectly puckered seams and a familiar plastic sheen. All three children immediately reach out to touch the sculpture. 'Don't!' I hiss, slapping at their fingers. A gallery guard is already coming towards us.

'What's the point of making metal look like plastic,' says the oldest, 'if you can't touch it to see it's not plastic?'

'It's partly about raising the banal, the everyday, to the level of high art,' I say. 'But it's also challenging our ideas about what art is supposed to …' I realize I'm alone. The children have disappeared into another room, in order to touch some sculptures. By the time I get to them the middle one is circling a stack of plastic chairs pierced by two seal-headed swimming rings, his fingers splayed. Another guard is following him round and round it, trying to keep his hands in sight.

'Let's look over here,' I say, grabbing the middle one. We now seem to have our own personal guard, silently shadowing us wherever we go. The children accept this escalation as a challenge.

'You distract her,' says the oldest to the middle one, 'and I'll touch the lobster when she's not looking.'

'No one is going to touch anything,' I whisper. 'Don't you have any sense of …' The three of them scoot ahead of me, and the guard passes by in pursuit. I catch up as they are bearing down on two blow-up turtles fixed to a chain-link fence, and gather them by their wrists.

'I think we've seen everything now,' I say, herding everyone towards the door. 'Time for ice cream.' As we reach the exit I find myself calculating the extent to which my children's behaviour can be blamed on my singular lack of authority, and how much of it is the fault of the artist Jeff Koons. A light rain is falling in the park.

'I actually brushed the caterpillar with the back of my hand on the way out,' says the oldest.

'What did it feel like?' I say.

'Metal,' he says.

For obvious reasons I prefer to do most of my child-rearing in private. I can do it in public if I have to, but it takes a lot out of me; parenting is largely a process of trial and error, and I don't like other people seeing the error part. Frankly, I find being in public on my own stressful enough, and for that reason I am only too happy to use my children as an excuse to stay in. Unfortunately this is not always possible.

Somewhere in my pre-Christmas clutch of invitations is one for a book launch. Although it is organized by friends of mine, I have already placed the event in a mental box marked 'optional'. This is because I don't know the author and because you never know how you are going to feel about going outside on a random day in the future.

I have forgotten all about the book launch when, a few weeks hence, with my wife away in Amsterdam, one of these friends rings in order to ensure my attendance that evening.

'I can't,' I say with what I hope sounds like dejection. 'I mean I would, but I've got the kids and no one to baby-sit.'

'Bring them,' she says. Her tone hints that non-compliance is not among the available alternatives.

'Really? OK, that sounds great.'

I scroll back through my inbox to find the details. The book is called *Once More with Feeling* and the launch is described as 'a festive evening of hymn and carol singing at St James's, Piccadilly'. I may as well extend my sons an invitation to be nit-combed.

'Guess what?' I say. 'We're going to a party, which won't end until past your bedtime.'

The three of them, still in their school uniforms, stare at me from the sofa.

'What sort of party?' asks the oldest.

'A book launch – there will be refreshments, though, and, um, a bit of carol singing.'

'Oh no!' screams the youngest, throwing himself to the floor.

'It'll be fun!' I say.

We are late, threading our way up Piccadilly through crowds of pedestrians with shopping bags. I have foolishly driven into central London and left the car in a car park whose charges took my breath away.

'Why is there singing at a book party?' asks the middle one.

'Well, the book's a collection of hymns and carols, so I guess they thought it would be appropriate to sing hymns and carols.'

'Hymns? You didn't say that before!'

'Exactly where is this thing happening?' asks the oldest.

'In a church,' I say.

They all stop walking.

'Oh my God,' says the middle one.

'Singing hymns in a church,' says the oldest. 'That is basically church.'

'You said we were going to a party!' screams the youngest, his eyeballs shining with fury. 'And you're taking us to church!'

'But there will be refreshments,' I say.

There are no refreshments. The youngest slumps with his forehead against the pew in front, staring at the floor. The oldest seems mildly impressed that one of the readers is Ian Hislop, whom he recognizes from *Have I Got News for You*. The middle one begins to sing along to the carols in spite of himself, while I repeat interesting facts I have gleaned from a pamphlet I found on my seat. 'This church was designed by Christopher Wren,' I whisper. For the moment, all is calm.

Afterwards I can think only about how much the car park is costing. The youngest one vanishes. The oldest drags the middle one away by the arm. 'I'm going to get him to say "Ian Hislop" in a loud voice when Ian Hislop goes by.'

'Don't do that,' I say. 'This is a church. William Blake was baptized here.'

'Who's Ian Hislop?' asks the middle one.

After ten minutes of searching I finally find the youngest one by the doors.

'Let's go, Dad,' he says, grabbing my hand.

'We need the other two,' I say, thinking about the car park.

'Where are they?'

'I don't know.' I try to walk against the tide of people leaving, but I can't move. Then I spot the pair of them, standing on a pew near the aisle. The middle one has a beatific expression on his face. He tilts back his head, opens his mouth wide and clearly pronounces the words 'Ian Hislop'. In the crowd I can just see Ian Hislop's unmistakable head, looking this way, looking that way.

\*   \*   \*

This is my Valentine's Day gift to my wife: a romantic long weekend at home for one. I am taking the children away for a few days so she can work and sleep and go to the cinema with people who are not me. I left her to make all the arrangements, right down to the taxi at the other end, but sitting on the Stansted Express with our bags crushing my feet, I still take some time to congratulate myself.

I have enough experience of the Stansted Express to know that it doesn't deserve the second part of its name. Even now it is crawling through North London, pausing for long periods, the drawn-out silences punctuated by incomprehensible apologies. It doesn't matter, I think, because we are so incredibly early. If this journey takes twice as long as it's meant to, we will still be at the airport before check-in opens. I look at my children, all staring into tiny screens, their faces alight with eerie concentration. There is, unusually, so little adrenaline in my system that I fall into a gentle sleep.

I am awoken by a sudden lack of forward momentum. As I open my eyes the lights go out and the air conditioning ceases to whir. Don't worry, I think. We are still so very, very early. After ten minutes the PA system buzzes to life. 'Sorry for the delay, ladies and gentlemen,' says a voice. 'Unfortunately, we have hit somebody, an individual who was intending to commit suicide.' I look at the oldest, who is sitting across from me and staring into his lap while tinny music leaks from his ears. I look at the youngest one, who is watching what the oldest has described as an 'amazingly inappropriate' episode of *Family Guy* on his brother's iPod, and laughing quietly. I look at the middle one, who is looking at me.

'Did you hear that?' he says.

'Yes,' I say. 'Don't tell the other two.' In the seat in front of us, a passenger is trying to explain the situation to a German couple, but they don't seem to get it. With the power off, the carriage quickly turns chilly.

Eventually, in response to a quizzical look from the oldest, I take a notepad from my bag and write, 'Someone jumped in front of the train' on it. He removes his earphones and watches policemen wander up and down the track. The other passengers conduct themselves with seemly reserve, talking in hushed tones into mobiles. There is no trouble when the snack trolley immediately runs out of everything.

After an hour it becomes apparent that we will not be moving for at least another hour. I ring my wife to ask, almost in a whisper, about the possibility of other flights, if necessary to other airports.

'There's one at six-thirty to Munich,' she says. 'If München is Munich. It is, isn't it?'

'Well, I'd always thought so,' I say, but it occurs to me that I once believed that Bayreuth was just an alternative spelling for Beirut. 'Now I'm not sure.'

The youngest one suddenly laughs out loud. He still has headphones on, and he is still watching *Family Guy*. His brother prods him in the shin.

'Do you actually even know what's going on?' he says. The youngest looks up.

'Yeah,' he says. 'A poltergeist comes and Stewie gets sucked into a portal.'

The man in front of us tells the Germans that this sort of thing happens once or twice a year. In fact, I discover later, this is the fourth 'fatality' on the Stansted line in two months.

The full sadness of it struck me only later in the evening, back home nine hours after setting off. Only then did I remember the conductor walking into our silent carriage to ask the trolley man for a coffee for the driver.

Now I think of it, the term 'trial and error' is a bit misleading when applied to fatherhood, because one is rarely in a position to adapt in response to mistakes. You can't just stop doing things because they keep going wrong; you're more or less required to carry on. You take your children to a restaurant, and it ends badly. A month later you try again, and it goes badly again. Over the long term you may begin to notice incremental improvements in the outcomes, but this is more to do with your children getting older than anything you're doing.

My wife's book group – of which she is a founder member – meets monthly in various locations, including, occasionally, our kitchen. The last time this happened I was away, so I'm not certain how the children and I are to be accommodated.

'What happens to us?' I ask while my wife arranges cheeses on a plate.

'Nothing,' she says. 'Just stay out of the kitchen, that's all. And don't let them shout swearwords on the stairs. Or fight. I don't want anyone running in covered in blood.'

When the women of the book club begin to arrive, I assemble all three boys in the sitting room.

'Put your shoes on,' I say. 'We're going out.' I take them to the Thai restaurant over the road. At my insistence, we order starters none of us has tried before. We chat about school, sport, politics and YouTube videos we've seen of people falling off things. The children, to my quiet astonishment, comport themselves with uncharacteristic maturity. They are polite. They are open-minded about some of the stranger dishes. They do not bicker, or complain, or knock over my beer while fighting over a dumpling. No one asks to play with my phone, or storms out leaving the word 'Arsehole!' hanging in the air.

The restaurant, almost empty on our arrival, fills up, mostly with groups of women, some of whom look over and smile. After a while I start to grow self-conscious, losing the drift of the conversation and beginning to see myself in the way I imagine these women see me: as an embattled single father bringing up three boys on his own, beautifully. When I occasionally catch one of their admiring glances, I try to acknowledge it wearing a modest, vaguely embarrassed expression that says, 'Yes, it has been a struggle, but it's been worth it. These kids mean everything to me.'

'Why don't you just shut up?' the youngest says to the oldest.

'Why don't you just fuck off?' the oldest says to the youngest.

'Can we have the bill?' I say to the passing waiter.

When we get home, the book club is still in session in the kitchen. We creep into the sitting room and I shut the door quietly behind us.

'It was a good dinner,' I say softly. 'We've expanded our repertoire to include starters four and seven, and I learned a lot about the many different ways a person can hurt himself skateboarding off a roof.'

'Whatever,' the youngest says, kicking off his shoes so they hit the window blinds and then diving face first into the sofa.

The middle one picks up the TV remote and points it at the screen. As the tail end of *Police, Camera, Action!* comes blaring into the room, he starts playing keepy-uppy with a dirty tennis ball. The oldest one is already sprawled on the other sofa with his laptop open under his chin like a sun reflector. Seizing the opportunity to check my email, I pull my phone from my pocket and turn my back to the noise.

At this point the door swings open. I glance up from my phone and see my wife, and behind her a group of rather elegant women in long coats, peering in. My wife gestures with one upturned palm, in the manner of a museum curator.

'Typical,' she says. 'Any time of day or night, if you open this door, this is the scene that greets you.'

I start to say something in protest, but then I see myself as the six smiling women framed in the door see me, and I decide to go with it.

One fine autumn day I elect to take my children to the grand opening of London's new mega-mall, because it is half-term and we need an activity, and because the mega-mall happens to be very near our house, which has not heretofore been very near anything. In fact, it is now our closest retail experience, our local forty-three-acre shop, and I want them to be familiar with it so that in future I can ask them to nip out and get me some Louis Vuitton luggage.

We are worried, however, that we might be underdressed for the occasion. Our shoes are muddy. The middle one is wearing a hoodie, which for all I know might disqualify him from entry. The youngest is sporting a huge cut above his blackened eye, the result of running into a friend while celebrating a goal with his shirt pulled over his head. We ditch the hoodie, change coats, wipe food from each other's faces.

As we walk along the road I try to set the mega-mall opening day in some sort of wider historical context, because we should really be going to a museum or something in half-term.

'This entire area was the site of the 1908 Franco-British Exhibition, the centrepiece of which was the dazzling White City,' I say, lowering my voice as we pass other pedestrians in case my facts are wrong.

'Is that why the Tube station is called White City?' the middle one asks, pointing.

'Yes,' I say. 'That is exactly why. They also held the 1908 Olympics here.'

'Dad,' the youngest says, 'remember on *Family Guy*, Stewie was like—'

'I'm talking. The last remaining exhibition halls were demolished to build the giant mall,' I say, 'a temple to capitalism.' As we pass the new Tube station I see the mayor of London, Boris Johnson, chatting to reporters. 'Look,' I say. 'There is the mayor of London, Boris Johnson.' The older two crane their necks appreciatively.

We enter the mega-mall just as Dannii Minogue opens the new branch of Next, and become caught up in the whirling vortex of the crowd trying to get a look at her. We ride escalators while consulting a map we were handed at the door. Eventually we end up on a balcony towering over the atrium. Three storeys below, flashbulbs are popping at the foot of a stage.

'The man now shaking hands with Boris Johnson,' I say, 'is Philip Green, the owner of the Arcadia group.'

'Who's that one?' the oldest asks.

'That,' I say, 'is Sir Stuart Rose, chairman of Marks and Spencer.'

'Ah,' he says. My children seem oddly intrigued by the proximity of fashion industry bigwigs.

'And that man, unless I'm mistaken, runs the—'

'Bye,' the youngest says suddenly, turning on his heel.

'Where are you going?'

'Anywhere,' he says, 'but here.' His sullen expression and cut eye make him look like someone in search of trouble.

'You can't wander around a giant mall by yourself,' I say. He stalks off defiantly to lean against a pillar twenty yards away, where I can just see him being quizzed by a succession of security guards.

The other two insist on waiting for the ribbon cutting. I begin to feel I have overplayed the historical significance of what is essentially the opening of a bunch of shops. People pile in around and behind us. Half an hour later, an orchestra starts playing. Boris Johnson makes a speech, but we can't make out the words, only the familiar harrumphing cadences. Finally I pull them away.

'This is a mall,' I say. 'Let's shop.' As we approach the youngest and his pillar, I can see that he is being questioned by yet another security guard. He answers, but the guard puts his hand to his ear, unable to hear anything above Leona Lewis singing below.

The boy leans towards the cupped ear. 'CELEBRATING A GOAL!' he shouts.

\* \* \*

I once made an incredibly realistic giant pencil, which my oldest son wielded as part of a Book Week costume, in the guise of a fictional character called the Number Devil.

Honestly, this pencil was amazing – it could have come straight from the props department of *The Borrowers*. I kept it around for years because I was so proud of it, and also because it was the perfect length for batting the TV aerial back into position whenever strong winds pushed it out of alignment, a dangerous chore that required me to clamber out of a third-storey window and up onto the flat roof at the back of the house. Getting back inside was even trickier – some dangling was required – and I usually spent at least ten minutes sitting on the edge of the roof contemplating unwanted outcomes before I got cold enough to go for it. It was during one of these periods of reflection that I realized what a macabre detail the giant pencil would add to reports of my death. It would probably be enough to upgrade my obituary to the status of quirky page four news item. After that I started using an old mop handle, and the pencil got thrown away.

The point is, I am good at making things. I approach creative tasks with a fussy precision you don't find in many eight-year-olds; above all I am proficient at damping down the childlike enthusiasm that causes children to be so rubbish at making things. For this reason I can sometimes be a difficult collaborator. Trust me – you don't want my help with your science project. You want me to do it for you.

Towards the end of the Easter holidays my wife starts finishing every statement with the words 'because I have done everything and you have done nothing'. I am left trying to recall even a brief period in the last fortnight when I had the opportunity to do nothing, but I'm too knackered to think.

It is the night before school starts.

'You are helping them with their eggs tonight,' says my wife. 'Because I have done everything and you have done nothing.' I know she is referring to the younger boys' Easter egg competition entries. The older of the two has already decorated an egg with the flags of many nations, and only needs me to paint a tiny red dragon in the centre of the Welsh flag. The younger one has painted his egg in the likeness of Ringo Starr – he hasn't done a bad job, considering that he neither knows nor cares what Ringo Starr looks like – and only needs me to help him construct a complete scale-model drum kit for the egg to sit behind.

After half an hour spent holding an empty loo roll tube and staring into space, I am suddenly struck by inspiration.

'We're going to need more of these,' I say. 'Bring me some glue and some wooden matches.' I look around, and see that I am alone in the kitchen. The boy has gone into the other room to watch television. I scream his name. He slouches into the kitchen and I explain my plan to use sections of loo roll to create the different drums – snare, floor tom, etc. – with glued-on matchsticks for legs.

'Or we could just use Sellotape,' he says.

'No, no,' I say. 'Glue.'

Over the course of the next two hours I have to keep reminding myself that this is not my last-minute school project; I am merely here to facilitate someone else's vision. I disguise my bursts of inventiveness with leading questions.

'Do we think we need some sort of base, some sort of sturdy cardboard base, to anchor the whole thing?' I say.

'Um, yeah,' says the boy.

'I agree,' I say. 'Brilliant.'

I find a tin of refried beans which, if Ringo Starr were a medium-sized egg, would be the perfect proportions for his bass drum, but it still has refried beans in it.

'We need this emptied immediately,' I say, handing it to my wife as she passes. 'Washed out, label off, open both ends.'

'I think you can probably manage that yourself,' she says. 'Because I have done everything and you have done nothing.'

'Wait!' I shout. 'We've changed our minds. Open one end only.'

The boy and I agree on a late innovation: pipe-cleaner arms holding toothpick drumsticks.

'So,' I say, 'should the arms be glued to the egg itself, do you think, or to the back of the cardboard stool?'

'The egg,' he says.

'I think the stool, and I'm going to explain why—'

'The egg.'

'You need to clear all this stuff off the table before supper,' says my wife. 'Which I've just made, again, by the way.'

'It will look as if they're glued to the egg,' I say, 'but it will be more structurally sound if we—'

'Because I do everything and you do nothing.'

'I'm doing this,' I say.

'The egg,' says the boy.

The final debate centres on who will write 'The Beatles' on the front of the bean-tin bass drum.

'I'll write it,' he says.

'OK,' I say. 'Good, yes, you write it.' I hand him the pen. He writes, 'THE BEA.'

'Actually, you write it,' he says, handing the pen back.

'I'll tell you what we could do,' I say. 'We could download an actual picture of the front of Ringo Starr's actual drum, and we could print it out and stick it on.'

'I think that's cheating,' he says.

'It's not cheating,' I say slowly, 'and I'm going to explain why.'

The next morning the Ringo Starr egg, carefully packaged for transport, goes off to school, and I decide that its hasty construction and our troubled father–son collaboration will make a charming *Guardian Weekend* column. Also I have a deadline, and nothing else has happened to me all week.

In my account I am rashly frank regarding the extent of my contribution, because I figure it's the only credit I will ever get for my work – indeed for any of my primary school projects.

But that Friday something happens that I don't expect: Ringo Starr is awarded first prize in the egg competition. I am quietly overjoyed, and also surprised. In ten years, none of my three children has ever won the egg competition. Even Joseph Cast Into The Pit By His Brothers, a biblical tableau produced by my oldest son under my unstinting micromanagement and requiring no fewer than seven eggs, failed to move the judges.

By an awful, if wholly foreseeable accident of scheduling, the column in which I had been so rashly frank regarding the extent of my contribution to my son's Easter egg competition entry appears in print on the day of the annual school Fun Run.

I am sitting on a picnic rug near the back leg of the Fun Run course, drinking coffee and trying not to catch anyone's eye. Another father of my acquaintance approaches.

'So,' he says, 'I understand you engineered a victory in the egg competition. Nice one.'

'I didn't know it was actually going to win,' I say.

'I heard you slipped in a Fabergé egg,' he says. 'That's the rumour.'

'It was an egg playing the drums,' I say, weakly.

From where I am sitting, I can see my wife circulating with a copy of the *Guardian Weekend* magazine, just in case any of the other parents have missed the column in which I was so rashly frank. She stands over them, pointing out relevant passages. Eventually she returns to our rug.

'Everyone's shocked,' she says.

'You're jealous,' I say, 'because you've never won anything.'

'That's a lie,' she says. 'I won for a Book Week costume. Captain Underpants.'

'You sent that child to school in his pants. In March.'

'And a bathing cap,' she says. 'It was brilliant.'

'Well, they can't take my prize away,' I say. 'He's already eaten the jellybeans.'

'Ooh,' she says. 'There's the headmistress. I'm going to show her.'

'Please don't do that,' I say, but she is gone. I watch my sons jog around cones, wondering how many relatives I'll have to invent to pad out their Fun Run sponsorship forms. I think back to a humiliating encounter with my seventh-grade science teacher, who felt he had reason to suspect that my project on The Causes And Symptoms Of Gum Disease did not spring from a private passion.

'Is your father a dentist or something?' he asked.

'Yes,' I replied, feebly. I have a sense of an unbroken line of academic corruption, passing from generation to generation.

'Look how many I've done,' says my son, pointing to the little stickers decorating the number on his front, each representing a completed lap.

'Wow,' I say. He turns to show me his back, on which he has a different number, equally studded with stickers. 'Where did you get that?'

'Someone gave me theirs. Can I have money for an ice cream?'

'You can't just appropriate someone's number,' I say. 'You're meant to run your own—' I stop, because I realize his only responsibility is to sponsors I have yet to invent.

'The headmistress would like a word with you,' my wife says.

Fortunately, the headmistress, who is holding the magazine my wife has lately presented to her, is smiling. I am smiling, too, as broadly as I can manage in the circumstances. It is ironic, the headmistress says, that this year they had gone out of their way to ensure that prizes went only to entries that were clearly the children's own work.

'That's a sort of double deceit,' my wife says, 'because he deliberately made it look like he didn't help.'

That's not true, I want to say. Yes, there was a certain deliberate naive quality, but that was just part of the effect, so the materials could be seen for what they were as well as for what they represented – a section of loo roll cardboard serving as a snare drum; arms that are still identifiable as pipe cleaners. It's about clarity of vision. It was never about the jellybeans.

I don't say this, though, because everyone is laughing, and I think it best to laugh along as realistically as possible.

# CHAPTER TWO

Did I teach my children to use the internet? I certainly don't remember offering any lessons or demonstrations. I first got online at some point in 1997, before two of my three sons were even born. My recollection of the web in those days is of a half-finished cyber-suburb, a construction site giving on to vast fields. There wasn't much to do, and there was hardly anyone around. And it was slow. For a long time, sending emails just seemed like a less reliable form of faxing.

In the early days I stood over my children when they used the internet, not because it was a threatening new environment, but because it was expensive. One thought twice before going online to seek information; it wasn't even that likely you'd find it, and it might turn out to be quicker and cheaper to drive to the library and ask someone. The internet was, first and foremost, a test of one's patience.

My children were eerily patient with it, which is why my supervision eventually became patchy. A six-year-old will wait all day for some stupid online game to load. I won't. The first hard evidence that my children were using my computer without my knowledge came from the computer itself.

You'll know what I mean by it, even though I had to look up the correct term: saved form data. It refers to those words and phrases you type into little boxes on your computer, which your computer then stores so it can helpfully offer them up as suggestions in the future. So, for example, whenever you type a 'T' into Google, you might be greeted with this list:

technical term remembering box suggest type in Google
Tim Dowling
Tim Dowling smug
Tim Dowling twat

That's what I get, anyway. None of us, I suspect, would care to be judged by his saved form data – I'm embarrassed for myself on a regular basis – but occasionally I am greeted by search terms I know I have never typed. Once, for instance, I typed a 'Y' into Google and was greeted with 'YouTube 10 most funneist goals'. It's a typical example of a clutch of unfamiliar search terms one might file under Poor Spelling Fails To Yield Desired Results, along with '1000 beast footballgames' and 'stange insturments'.

When my children were small they were permitted to use my work computer under circumstances that numbered precisely zero, but I knew that if they wished to access the internct when they were supposed to be asleep, my office was easy to get to without being detected.

The discovery of this unfamiliar saved form data prompted me to sift through the search terms left on both computers – mine and my wife's – to see if I could gain any insight into my children's internet habits. If this sounds like spying, let me say in my defence that I was really bored that day. I went through the whole alphabet.

Most of the searches were more or less what you would expect: 'fantasy football'; 'hamster in a blender'. Some were mildly mysterious. The cryptic phrase 'brought me out of bed for this shrit' seemed to me to be one child complaining to another – typing it out softly, so as not to wake anyone – that a website he'd been woken up to view was proving insufficiently diverting.

Then I got to 'm' and up popped 'my Dad is an island'. For a long moment I forgot to breathe in. I am familiar with virtually every sentence on the internet that features both my name and the word twat, but nothing I've seen chilled me as much as 'my Dad is an island'. What did it mean?

I tried to imagine one of my sons sneaking up to the computer in the middle of the night to tap 'my Dad is an island' into Google. Why would a child do that? It makes no sense, I thought. And then I thought: it makes no sense to you, because you are an island.

Google was no help. I got no meaningful results for 'my Dad is an island'. The sentence did not exist anywhere on the World Wide Web. I couldn't stop thinking of my youngest son, the most likely suspect, trying to phrase his tearful query without using the word 'aloof', which he doesn't know, or 'unreachable', which he can't spell. 'My Dad,' he writes, alone in the dark, 'is an island.' There are zero results.

When he gets home from school the next day, I ask him to come with me. His oldest brother, intrigued by my artificially breezy tone, follows us. On the way upstairs I explain about saved form data, and by way of a warm-up I type a 'b' in the box. Up pops the phrase 'brought me out of bed for this shrit'.

'What does this mean?' I ask.

He looks a bit sheepish. 'You know they have those shirts that say, "You got me out of bed for this?" I just really wanted one.'

'Oh,' I say. 'Well, what about this?' I press 'm'.

He peers at the sentence 'my Dad is an island' and starts laughing. 'What the hell!' he says. 'I didn't write that.'

'That was me,' says his brother. 'I was looking for a book of poems we read in primary school. For Mum to put it in her bookshop.'

'But you get zero results,' I say.

'I know,' he says. 'It's actually called *Daddy Island*.'


Over time my children and the various machines in my life came to control and manipulate me in much the same way. The children realize I do not fully understand the machines. The machines seem to know that I do not fully understand the children. The children and the machines take it in turns to misbehave wilfully at critical times. Occasionally, when I send a child's phone thirteen unanswered 'where r u??' texts, only to receive the cryptic reply 'wots good cuz' four hours later, I feel they are acting in concert.

I am spending a long, lazy afternoon trying to print something for my wife. The printer, which has not worked properly for some time, refuses to spit out anything legible. I clean the printhead, put in new ink cartridges, clean the printhead again, deep clean the printhead, and manually realign the printhead, printing a new copy between each step, but they all come out the same: ridged, smudged, squashed.

Frustrated, I give up and go downstairs, where I am ineluctably drawn to the television. There isn't anything on. My wife walks into the room and sits down.

'Busy day?' she says.

'I just wanted to check the tennis,' I say. 'But there isn't any tennis yet.'

'Did you print out the thing I sent you?' she says.

'No,' I say. 'I tried, but I couldn't.'

We watch the Queen arriving at Wimbledon for the first time since 1977. My wife is weirdly excited by this, while I am unaccountably pissed off on Wimbledon's behalf.

'I love the Queen,' my wife says.

'I'd be like, oh, thanks for turning up,' I say. 'How did we manage without you for the last thirty-odd years.'

'Leave her alone,' my wife says. The screen freezes, with the Queen wearing a fixed grin that cannot hide her contempt for tennis. I push the remote and the screen goes blue. Nothing I own works.

'Arghh!' says my wife. 'Fix it!'

'I can't,' I say. 'We need a child.'

That afternoon I go to pick up the oldest one, wondering how many questions I should ask about his school trip before I raise the subject of the blank blue screen. As I drive, my phone pings and buzzes continually in my pocket, ten, fifteen, twenty times. Finally I pull over. It transpires that the phone is logged into the middle one's Facebook account and that I am receiving a stream of comments about a photo from the whole of Year 7. All the machines in my life are working against me, I think, or in the service of others. This eventuality was probably predicted by somebody. I should have read more science fiction.

The next day is bright and sunny, the hottest of the year so far.

'What are we going to do today?' my wife asks.

'I'm going to buy a new printer.'

'I wish you'd buy me a printer,' she says.

'I'm going to get a printer for both of us,' I say. 'A wireless printer that will print everything from everywhere.'

'Really?'

'I think so.'

The printer I end up buying is black and twice the size of the old one. It looks like Darth Vader's head. I carry it up to my office, where I spend a sweltering half-hour crawling around under my desk with wires. The configuration process is meant to be straightforward, but it's not, and I have to back up and start again a few times. Then I go downstairs and repeat the process on my wife's computer, which is a different make and requires a different installation procedure.

Finally, with the afternoon gone, I find a picture of the dog on my wife's computer and press Print. Nothing seems to happen, but when I go up to my office a picture of the dog is waiting in the printer tray, richly coloured and exquisitely detailed. It's a miracle.

'Look,' I say, showing it to the oldest one.

'Did you just print that?' he says.

'I printed it,' I say, 'from downstairs.'

'Whoa,' he says.

The next day, I'm at my desk looking up the word 'ineluctably' to make sure I don't really mean 'inexorably', when the printer beeps and grinds into life. Oh my God, I think.

What have I done? I didn't even touch anything! I watch as it sucks a sheet of paper into its belly and judders with such force that it rocks the spindly little table I've set it on.

The piece of paper slides out and lands on the floor. I pick it up. It says, 'HI DAD' on it. It knows me, I think. It knows it's mine.

Late at night I creep up to my office to check my email before bed. I should know by now that emails of promise rarely hit one's inbox after 11 p.m., but one can dream.

While trying to delete some fresh junk mail I hit an unknown combination of keys with a fat thumb and the computer starts to read its screen to me.

'Subject – mega deal on drill bits and power files,' it says, in a loud robot voice.

'Sorry?' I say.

'Reply to no reply at tool shop direct dot co dot UK.'

'Shut up,' I say, clicking the mouse repeatedly. I try to turn down the volume, but pressing the mute key only makes the screen scroll upwards.

'So now you've changed what the buttons mean?' I say.

'Please read,' it says. 'A personal appeal from Wikipedia founder Jimmy Wales.'

'Oh my God,' I say, kneading the keyboard with my fists. 'Are you planning to say the entire internet?' It ignores me and carries on. I go to bed, shutting my office door tightly behind me.

The next morning the computer is still talking. I try to ignore it and get down to work, but the voice starts saying every letter I type. When I hit the space bar, it says, 'Space'. After an hour of this, I do what I have to do.

'Help!' I scream.

'What do you want?' says the oldest one, who is drifting past the door in his pyjamas, laptop open under his chin.

'Please consider the environment before printing this email,' says the computer.

'I can't live like this,' I say. 'Make it stop.'

'Command F5,' says the boy, somehow managing to roll his eyes without peeling them from the screen.

'Voiceover off,' says the computer.

'Thank you,' I say. 'That was really beginning to …' The boy is already gone.

A morning like any other: I go up to my computer and jab the space bar to make it come to life. Only it doesn't. I wait a while, trying to determine how much unsaved work lies beyond the black screen. Eventually impatience overrides caution and I turn the computer off and then back on again. Except it doesn't come back on.

I breathe in slowly. I tell myself it's too early to panic over the possibility of catastrophe. I only really care about one thing on my present computer, the aforementioned unsaved work. For the sake of argument, let's call it a nearly completed book. I do sort of need that. I turn the computer off and on again, but there is not much difference between the two.

I'm not an idiot. I email the updated document to myself at intervals precisely in case this sort of thing happens. My priority is to find the most recent version and secure it on another computer.

Except that the most recent email for some reason contains only the first quarter of the document. The newest complete version in my inbox is months old. It turns out I am an idiot after all. Now, I tell myself quietly, you may panic.

I shriek for the middle one, forcing him from his bed. He comes downstairs, stares into space as I carefully explain the situation so far, taps the space bar, clicks the mouse, and tries a few odd keystroke combinations.

'Dunno,' he says finally.

'What?' I say.

Three days and a dozen helpline calls later, no one in my family is speaking to me. My throat is sore from shouting. My knee and left fist hurt from hours spent pounding one with the other. My children have seen a side of me I have never wanted to show them: panicked, irrational, brimming over with uncontrolled fury. They've seen it before, to be fair; just not this many days in a row.

My hard drive is in the possession of a man in Wandsworth who isn't returning my calls, possibly because of the tone of my voice in all the messages I keep leaving. My wife rings from the M3, her idea of a safe distance.

'Any luck?' she asks.

'No,' I say, trying out a new tone of giddy resignation. 'My life is ruined, but whatever. That's cool.'

'Gotta go,' my wife says.

'Me, too,' I say. 'I have another call.'

It's Darren from Data Solutions, ringing to let me know that my hard drive is unreadable, and quite possibly blank.

'OK, Darren,' I say. 'That's cool.'

I hang up and start searching through all my inboxes and outboxes again, trying different keywords. A draft email I've never seen before suddenly pops up: a complete, unsent version of the document from five days before.

'I found you,' I say. Unfortunately I can't think of anyone to ring who would, at this point, be pleased for me. Not even Darren.

A week later, I walk into the kitchen to find the oldest one striding back and forth, phone to ear, panting in quiet fury. His bank card has been stolen, thieves have exceeded his overdraft and he's been cut off mid-call, twice.

'Yes, I'm still here,' he says. 'I already … yes, it … wait … can you hear me now?' He stalks out of the room in search of better reception.

'Remind you of anyone?' my wife says.

'I don't know what you're talking about,' I say.

There is a bloodcurdling scream from next door and the oldest returns, his face dark purple.

'Holy fucking shitting God!' he shouts, lifting the phone high over his head. His behaviour is, I must admit, eerily familiar, particularly the way he adjusts his run-up to ensure that, when he finally hurls the phone, it lands softly on the sofa. Then he stomps back out.

'Attractive, isn't it?' my wife says.

I don't answer, because secretly the boy's response strikes me as wholly proportionate. I mean, what else are you supposed to do?

A fortnight later the middle one walks into my office, iPad to nose, to turn the wireless router on and off. He finds me looking intently at a leaflet titled 'About Your Recovery'.

'From alcohol?' he asks.

'No,' I say. 'From data loss.'

'Oh,' he says.

'What do you mean, "from alcohol?"' I say.

The boy shrugs and walks off, pausing only to scrutinize the blinking light on the front of the router on his way out of the door.

In the weeks since I lost all my data, my computer's dead hard drive has been on a journey. It's now in a clean room in Surrey, where people in hairnets and disposable over-shoes are awaiting a decision from me. Along with my leaflet, I've received a two-page report estimating the likely percentage of my data that can be recovered: most, if not all, but possibly none. The enormous cost, on the other hand, is not an estimate; nor is it refundable, nor does it include VAT.

My computer has been on a different journey. For an incredibly modest price, it has been fitted with a one-terabyte hard drive and returned to me, blank as new. A certain amount of data has migrated back: 12,000 old emails pinged into my inbox, and all my music purchases reappeared. But otherwise it's empty. When I turn on my computer in the morning, I feel strangely unencumbered, and correspondingly susceptible to notions of promise. I begin to think that my old data should stay lost.

My wife, meanwhile, is trying to convince me that recovery is something I should seriously consider, whatever the cost.

'We're still talking about my hard drive, right?' I say, jamming an empty wine bottle nose-first into the recycling bin.

'Yes,' she says. 'What about all your old documents, things you've written?'

'Don't need it,' I say. 'Chances are I'd never look at it again anyway.'

'It's a legitimate business expense,' she says, knowing how favourably disposed I am towards language that makes me sound like a businessman.

'Who cares?' I say. 'I'm free!'

Some days later, at an event in Sussex, a strange woman starts showing me pictures of her dog on her phone.

'I have dogs,' I say, whipping out my own phone in retaliation. As I scroll through to find the most charmingly composed picture of the pair, four years' worth of memories flash before my eyes: red-eyed holiday snaps; accidental shots of the kitchen door; a blurry, vertiginous pap of Phil Tufnell taken by one of my children; photos of Halloween costumes, snake eggs, a snowman wearing 3D glasses, my new ladder, a patch of lawn ringed by the shoes of fellow party guests ... Suddenly all this stuff – this digital information on which so many fragile memories are pinned, and which exists nowhere but on my old, cracked-screen phone – seems terribly important to me. My data is my memory, and I am as anchored as I am imprisoned by it.

A week later I receive in the post a black box no bigger than a cigarette packet: the contents of my old hard drive. I plug it into my computer and have a look. As far as I can tell, everything is there: half-finished articles, old invoices, a jpeg of a Mondeo starter motor, the Beach Boys' *Greatest Hits*. It would be the work of seconds to transfer the lot to my new, giant hard drive. In the end, I decide to keep it all on the black box, in case I one day feel the need to chuck it into a canal.

## Lessons in primatology 1

Over the course of a decade of writing about family life, I have from time to time experienced what military strategists might call blowback. It can be subtle: a slight but perceptible decline in my wife's amusement at being portrayed as a harridan in the national press. One of my children may object to having his words reported in a way that he believes misrepresents him somehow, even after he's spent the fiver.

Obviously I regret causing offence or embarrassment – it's not my primary motivation – but on those occasions when I accidentally overstep the mark, a larger problem presents itself: next week's deadline. Having pissed my family off this Saturday, how do I write about them the following one? On those difficult occasions I simply opt for a temporary blurring of identities, a minor precaution which protects the sensibilities of all concerned, and rarely undermines the essential truth of what has transpired.

So, for example, my life partner – let's call him Sean – might arrive home of an evening with our three adopted ex-research chimps. It's Friday, we're both tired, and there is no food in the house.

'One of us,' Sean says glumly, 'is going to have to go to Sainsbury's.'

'Don't worry,' I say sweetly, 'I'll go.'

'Oh,' Sean says, 'I didn't expect that.'

Sean has failed to remember that today is our gay-wedding anniversary, and I have not reminded him. Sean is normally good on dates, because he writes things down, but for some reason he is never able to remember our anniversary. I think he resents the obligation to commemorate a day we both found fairly traumatic. Some years I also forget, but this morning my eye snagged on the date in the newspaper, and I knew it had some significance.

All day I have been plotting how best to take advantage of this. At first I toyed with the idea of organizing some kind of surprise evening out, until I realized that anything that elaborate might make Sean feel terrible, when I wanted him to feel only mildly derelict. I thought of going out to buy some monstrously expensive present, but Sean is difficult to buy for, possessing both particular tastes and a charming inability to hide his disgust. In any case, I spent all afternoon googling myself and missed the shops.

A trip to the supermarket suddenly seemed the perfect answer – a card, some cheap flowers and a bottle of champagne – just enough to say that I care, more than you.

As I unpack the shopping, Sean catches me in the kitchen.

'What are you doing behind there?' he says. 'What are you hiding?'

'Nothing.'

'What is that? You bought flowers?'

'Yes,' I say, holding them up. 'But then I thought you might think they were hideous.'

'No, those are nice,' he says. 'I like them, thank you.'

As he takes them from me and goes off in search of a vase, I realize this might be the time to come clean, but I find I am not man enough to relinquish the upper hand. I go upstairs and puzzle over what to write in the card. I want something simple and not overly romantic, maybe something amusing like 'To a very civil partner'. In the end I just write 'It's OK that you forgot', and stuff it in an envelope marked 'Sean'.

A little later, Sean comes in while I am cooking. 'What's this?' he says, picking up the envelope. As he opens it I retrieve the bottle of champagne from the freezer.

'Uh-oh,' he says. 'I forgot.'

'I knew you would,' I say, kissing him gently on the cheek. 'You always do.'

'You came in with flowers, and still I didn't get it,' he says. 'That's really bad.' Our youngest chimp, Kurt, waddles into the room and makes the sign for 'hungry'.

'Dad fooled me,' Sean tells him. 'It was our anniversary, and I forgot.'

'Again,' I say. Kurt makes the sign for 'whatever', helps himself to a banana and leaves. I pour the champagne.

'I notice you got only a half-bottle,' Sean says.

'I know you don't really like it,' I say. 'It seemed a waste.' Our middle chimp, Anton, comes in and signs, 'Can I have some of that?'

'You can have a sip of mine,' Sean says. 'I don't really like it.'

'Just a sip,' I say. I worry about giving Anton alcohol, because he's only ten and he can lift a car.

# CHAPTER THREE

In the beginning, I throw the child a ball. It bounces off his head, and he tips over. His mother comes in to see why he is crying.

'He fell over,' I say, careful not to look at the spot where the ball has ended up.

A little later, when the child can walk, I take him outside and kick the ball to him. He tries to kick it back, and he tips over. I pick him up, retreat a short distance with the ball and start again. This carries on for years marked by little discernible progress. In the meantime another son comes along, then another. I bounce balls off their heads in turn.

Then one day in the park I notice all three of them are performing strange manoeuvres with the ball, little feints and sleights of foot named for the players who first popularized them, players I've never heard of because I am American and know nothing about football. I don't even call it football.

The children did not exist when these legendary footballers were playing, and yet their celebrated manoeuvres have somehow been passed down to them over my head. My primary feeling is one of relief.

They introduce me to games I don't understand; school-yard versions of football for four or fewer players, with rules that seem designed to work against me. Even though I am larger, I find it difficult to take the ball off them, and the pointless running is exhausting. Eventually I am relegated to permanent goalkeeper, positioned between two piles of coats, piles which I surreptitiously move closer together when no one is looking.

'Dad, come on,' shouts my son as I let in another goal. 'You're being useless.' He is not teasing me; nor is he crowing. He is furious that my inability to defend is affecting the delicate balance of a one-on-one game between him and his younger brother. He has a much sterner accusation in reserve – that I am not even trying – but he knows me well enough. In my own pathetic way I am doing my best.

The extent to which a parent is competitive with children depends largely on how competitive you are in the first place. Many dads, including me, have virtually no experience of winning at games until they start thrashing their own tiny children. This is how I finally learned to enjoy ping-pong. You may pretend to yourself that you are teaching them to be good losers, but they are also learning how to be smug and graceless winners. Trust me: when the time comes, they will remember.

It has always seemed strange to me that children are traditionally introduced to the notion of competition via the cruellest game ever devised by man: Snakes and Ladders. Defeat is often crushing, and because it's a game of chance there is no plausible way for parents to engineer a less painful outcome. After the second time the children land themselves at the top of a twisting snake you look into their little brimming eyes, even while you're stepping your own piece up another ladder, and you tell them that it's nothing to be upset about: this is just how games work. And also, by the way, how life works.

I was, frankly, quite content to suck at football, relieved to put the complex question of father–son competition behind me as soon as possible, and to step warily into the role of spectator.

When I was very small, I spent a lot of Sundays in a field watching my father play touch football, a slightly less violent version of American football. One of my earliest memories is of standing on the touchline on a crisp, autumn afternoon, aged about three, and having a motor-cycle fall on top of me. The incident left me with a certain ambivalence towards spectatorship. At that point I never imagined I would have children who would one day be forced to watch me play sport. Which is just as well, because this never came to pass.

Instead, it is Sunday and I am standing on a touchline watching my middle son play football, in one of about twenty matches taking place on an open expanse of ground. I am dressed for the unseasonable weather, but I'm still cold, and I can see I'm going to have to give up my gloves at half-time: the middle one is playing with the ends of his sleeves bunched in his fists.

I've maintained a semi-regular presence at matches across the season, regular enough so that other fathers will occasionally come up and chat, but not so regular that they've realized I never have any idea what they're talking about. One of them approaches and nods when he gets close.

'They're struggling today,' he says.

'Yeah,' I say. 'It's really muddy.'

As I speak, a well-aimed ball adheres to the ground just short of the goal, forcing the keeper to wade out and pull it free. I feel I have made a point worth making.

'A few players missing,' he says. 'They've had to mix things up. That one, he's never played at right back.'

'Really? Where does he usually play?' I ask.

'He's the keeper,' he says.

'So who's that in goal then?'

'The other keeper.'

'Of course,' I say. 'This mud. Honestly.'

At half-time I wander over to another match, where the youngest one is playing and my wife is watching, with the dog sitting beside her. She hands me the lead as I approach. 'What's happening over here?' I say.

'They've just started,' she says. 'There was a delay because both teams showed up in the same kit, so someone had to go and get bibs.'

'What's the score?'

'No idea,' she says.

'It's two-one,' says another father, thumbing at his BlackBerry. 'Just doing my report for the local paper.'

'They're playing ever so well,' my wife says. 'Aren't they?'

'I'll say your boy was solid at the back,' the father says. '"Despite his diminutive stature, Dowling maintained a solid defensive presence for the" … Oh dear.' A whistle blows.

'What happened?' I say. The youngest one jogs past, his face contorted with frustration and fury.

'Never mind!' the other father shouts at him. 'Foul throw,' he says to me. 'They've been doing it all day. If they'd just learn to plant themselves, they'd be fine.'

'Yeah,' I say. 'Sorry, but I have no idea what you're talking about.'

'Throw-ins,' he says. 'You've got to keep both feet on the ground.' I feel a twinge of embarrassment: even my children don't know that I don't know this.

'How's the other match going?' the father asks. I look at the ground and shake my head ruefully.

'It's really muddy over there,' I say.

At half-time I return to the first match, where several fathers are indulging in a pastime that often crops up when we're losing badly: debating the ages of the other team's players.

'Look at number seven,' one says. 'He's never thirteen – look at his calves.'

'It's a scandal,' says another, as number 7 scythes through our defence. Obviously there is a broad developmental range at this age, with everybody either side of puberty, but I know better than to mention it.

'Shocking,' I say.

'It's a scandal,' the first father says. 'He's at least seventeen!'

'Number twenty-four is even bigger,' the linesman says.

'Yeah, the midfielder,' another father adds. 'He's not on the pitch. Where's he gone?'

'He probably had to take his kids to the zoo,' the first father says. Number 7 churns his way past us, a colossus beset by elves. His foot catches, and he drops to one knee as the ball sinks into the mire. A small boy runs up, works it free and boots it over the halfway line.

'Mud,' I say, 'is a great leveller.'

For me the most difficult form of spectatorship revolves around the professional game, where I must watch alongside my children. I can follow a football match on television – I'm even interested – but I have no gift for armchair punditry, and none of the passion of a true supporter. With every fresh attempt to join in, I manage to say something that reveals a whole new facet of my ignorance.

I have had to promise my youngest son that he will have first claim on the next one-on-one father–son opportunity to present itself – he has been sorely short-changed in favour of his older brothers – but after months of waiting, he has given up and taken matters into his own hands. He has won two tickets to a football match.

They come courtesy of an Arts Council initiative called Kick Into Reading. Far from lavishing funding on one-legged Lithuanian dance troupes, as the Tories fear, the Arts Council is wisely spending money on a project that teaches kids that literacy and football are, if not exactly indivisible, at least not mutually exclusive, through a combination of storytelling and free tickets to see QPR play Hull City.

My sons are all Chelsea fans, but I have for some time harboured a desire to transfer a portion of our familial allegiance to Queens Park Rangers. Because their stadium is within walking distance of our house and the tickets are cheaper than those at Chelsea, I have argued that we might participate more fully in the life of the less top-flight club. I am American, however, and fully conscious of the fact that

I have no idea what I am talking about. I routinely defer to the older two on football matters, and they assure me that QPR tickets are easy to come by because QPR are rubbish. But the youngest has never been to a match and is blissfully unaware of Rangers' position deep in the bottom half of the table of an altogether different league. He might yet be converted.

Over the course of Saturday, his mood veers wildly: one minute he wants to leave for the stadium two hours early, the next he is insisting that he doesn't want to go at all. Like me, he has trouble savouring anticipation of the unknown. It is, however, a sunny stroll to Loftus Road and he has cheered up considerably by the time we get there. In the meantime I have become increasingly apprehensive. The sign above the turnstile reads 'Supporters Only'. There is no sign saying 'Dads Who Like A Bargain'. I feel like an impostor.

The boy is not so self-conscious. He may be the only eight-year-old in history who has been told to be quiet at a football match. I can sympathize with the elderly woman in front of us, who had to endure him shouting, 'WE! ARE! QPR!' in her ear for forty-five minutes, and I understand why she might eventually feel the need to turn around and suggest that he draw breath. Perhaps I should have admonished him myself, but I don't know the etiquette, and given that the crowd behind us is loudly accusing the Hull City supporters of indulging a fondness for anal intercourse – to the tune of, I think, 'Go West' – his behaviour strikes me as being within local limits of acceptability.

By the second half he has learned to flap his seat up and down to make a supportive thudding noise, and he is so irritated with my efforts to calm him down that he insists on switching places with a schoolfriend's mother. After that I wash my hands of his hysteria, and try to come up with authentic-sounding things to shout. The old woman, I notice, contents herself with an occasional 'Come on, Rs!', but this is a little intimate for me. My mind begins to wander, and when QPR score early in the second half I accidentally shout, 'Kick into reading!' I resolve thereafter to confine myself to clapping.

By the end I realize I'm never going to master the rites and rhythms of fandom. Then I think: who cares? They won 2-0. We're on our way!

One Sunday I come downstairs to find the middle one typing furiously on a laptop while a football match roars from the television. The middle one's friend is leaning over his shoulder, staring at the screen. I lean in, too.

'What are you doing?' I ask.

'I'm providing live match commentary on Twitter,' he says.

'But you're not on Twitter,' I say.

'I know,' he says. 'I just joined for this.' I watch as he types, 'tottenham break with lennon but cross is poor.'

'How many followers do you have?' I say.

'None,' he says.

'That means no one can see your commentary,' I say. 'You're typing into thin air.'

'Whatever,' he says, typing into thin air.

'You're slightly missing the point of ...' I stop there, realizing anything I say about Twitter will eventually be proved idiotic. Instead I take out my phone, log in to Twitter and announce his odd enterprise. I read the tweet back to him.

'My son has set up a Twitter account so he can—'

'Don't say I'm your son!' he shouts. 'I need credibility! Say I'm a work colleague!'

'Too late.' Within minutes he has twelve followers. Unfortunately, most of them arrive just as he tweets the words, 'Screw this I'm bored.'

'You can't stop now,' I say. 'I recommended you!' Shortly after that, he loses half his new followers by announcing a goal when there is no goal. At half-time I tweet from the kitchen to tell him lunch is ready.

Sunday lunch is often taken in front of televised sport, but because the middle one has a friend staying, we are going out of our way to seem convivial. We eat together in the kitchen, off plates, and attempt to converse intelligently about the point of Twitter.

'I don't really understand it,' my wife says.

'My brother joined and then he tweeted that my mum was his best friend,' the middle one's friend says.

'How lovely,' my wife says.

'Um, I think he was being ironic,' the middle one says.

'I'm sure he wasn't,' my wife says, before turning to the youngest one. 'I'm your best friend, aren't I?'

'Not really,' he says.

'But you'll look after me in my old age. And stay with me always.'

'I'm going to have a bachelor pad,' he says.

'What about me?' I say. 'Who's going to look after me?'

'You'll probably die first anyway,' the youngest one says.

'Yes,' I say, 'but I'm planning to be ill for a long time before that.'

'Then I would just get bored and pull the plug on you,' he says. There follows a protracted and uncomfortable silence.

'You've ruined lunch,' I say. 'Get out.'

'Fine,' he says, beaming. He is already standing, ready for his exit.

'I'm going to be such a burden to you,' I say.

'Bye,' he says.

'Two minutes till the second half,' the middle one says, opening the laptop by his side.

'Lunch's duration isn't dictated by the FA's timetable,' I say.

'I can't believe how slowly you eat,' my wife says.

'What are you talking about?' I say. 'I've eaten exactly as much as you.'

'No, you haven't. I'm nearly done.'

'Right,' I say. 'I'm going to weigh our plates. Give me yours.'

'Let go,' she says, making a stabbing motion with her fork. The middle one and his friend take advantage of the distraction to leg it. My wife's phone rings and she goes off in search of it. Alone at the table, I pull out my own phone. There is a new tweet from the middle one. It says, 'AND WERE BACK.'

My oldest son is sitting in front of the television with his mother, watching the start of the England–Ukraine match. As the camera tracks along the England line-up during the national anthem, my wife says things like, 'Oooh, I like him!' or 'He's nice!' When it passes across the face of Ashley Cole, she says, 'He's been a naughty boy!'

If I were at home, I would look at my son and we would both roll our eyes. But tonight I am not at home. I'm at Wembley with the middle one. We're surrounded by thousands of men with shaved heads, all of them singing 'God Save the Queen' with alarming gusto. I cannot see the line-up on the field because I am holding up a bit of red card that forms a tiny part of the cross in an enormous England flag spreading across one end of the stadium. In many ways this is a perfectly ordinary father–son outing. In other ways, it's one of the weirdest experiences I've ever volunteered for.

After the national anthem, my wife rings.

'Where are you? Is it exciting?'

'Behind the goal, and a bit up.'

'Are you making it special for him?' she says.

'Yes, I am,' I say.

She hangs up. I turn to the boy and shout, 'This is great!' but he's looking down at the field. I follow his eyes. John Terry knocks into a Ukrainian player with long, tied-back blond hair, and the Ukrainian goes down. Everyone around us boos.

'Who's that?' I ask.

'Voronin,' the boy says.

'Get up, My Little fucking Pony!' shouts a man behind me. I am surrounded by people who believe the Ukrainian player is feigning injury, even though he clearly isn't. It's all very well being patriotic, I think, but his nose is bleeding.

At a Premiership match I can usually get away with clapping when everyone else claps, standing up when everyone else stands up and shaking my head ruefully when the situation appears to warrant it, but this is my first international and I'm finding it very difficult to belt out 'Rule, Britannia!' with my arms held above my head in a giant V. It's not just because I'm American; I don't know any of the words to 'Rule, Britannia!' beyond the first two. In principle I find this sort of passion admirable, or at least interesting. Up close, it strikes me as undiplomatic, and a little embarrassing.

Not knowing what to do with myself, I scan the crowd for a role model. Eventually I find him a few seats down the row: a man with a beard who sits with his arms folded, shouting nothing, singing nothing. I decide to imitate him for the rest of the match. When Terry scores late in the second half, I do not join in the hostile, saliva-spraying chorus of 'You're Not Singing Any More' directed at the drooping Ukrainian flags.

'It doesn't really work,' my son says, 'because they don't know we're singing about them not singing.'

I look at him with folded arms and one raised eyebrow, and I nod.

On Saturday evening, there is a sudden outbreak of family harmony that spreads through the house like a virus. One minute I am lying face down on the sofa trying to ignore the terrible television programme I have deliberately chosen to watch, the next I am sitting in the kitchen with my wife and children, laughing and helping to prepare a deeply odd supper made from ingredients we already happen to own. Before we eat, we take a short break to run round the park with the dogs, in the dark, chasing each other and shrieking with delight.

I can attribute this unscheduled merriment to a single cause: it's the snow. At about 5 p.m., I turned on the outdoor light to show everyone the white flakes pelting the back garden, and the mood instantly lifted. Snow fixes everything.

It also helped, I suppose, that the oldest one was at a friend's house. Outbreaks of harmony invariably coincide with one of the children being missing – it doesn't matter which one. This might lead a non-parent to conclude that three children is too many and two the perfect number, but it doesn't work like that. You have to have the extra one to get the benefit of its absence. Anyway, it was my expressed intention to cite a single cause, and I chose snow.

The goodwill brought about by the snow survives the oldest one's return, and the night, and lunch with friends the next day. In fact, it lasts nearly twenty-four hours, until a wave of severe ill-feeling overtakes us, followed by bouts of swearing, hot tears, an interval of door-slamming and a brief period of my wife screaming, 'I will not live like this!' before changing into her pyjamas prematurely.

This descent into discord also has a single attributable cause: Chelsea. During the car ride back from lunch, their lead over Manchester United dwindles from 3-0 to 3-1 to 3-2.

'Turn it off!' the middle one shrieks, kicking the seat-back in fury.

'I'm listening,' I say. 'Don't be such a—'

'Oh my God, they're rubbish!'

One of my failings as a father – from my children's point of view – is my inability to summon up strong feelings about sport in general and Chelsea in particular. I don't personally consider it a failing; I prefer to see it as evidence of a healthy sense of perspective. When I greet two opposition goals with a stoicism bordering on indifference, I feel I am leading by example. Or, as my wife would put it, 'doing nothing, as usual'.

We arrive home in time to see Man U score a third, after which all hell breaks loose. My wife has an extremely low tolerance for high feeling engendered by televised football. An argument ensues, and the older two storm off before the end of the match, slamming doors and punching walls. I'm left with the youngest one, who is standing next to me emitting a sound like a kicked dog.

'You have to speak to them,' my wife says.

'I will,' I say, 'but there's, like, four minutes of added time.'

I don't say anything until supper, which has been repeatedly postponed on account of the pork being, in my opinion, dangerously underdone. The children eat in cautious silence, fearing I will suddenly declare the meal unsafe and collect all the plates again.

'Perhaps,' I say finally, 'the time has come for you to withdraw your support for Chelsea.'

'You have no idea what you're talking about,' the oldest says.

'It's not your fault,' I say. 'You were born into a generation unfamiliar with disappointment.'

'I've only ever been disappointed,' he says.

'Just accept that your emotional investment in a bunch of underperforming millionaires was a regrettable mistake,' I say. 'You have no ancestral history of support, no one to betray. You can just walk away.'

The children stare at me for a minute. The middle one stands up and slaps his forearms.

'You cut me open, I bleed blue!' he shouts, marching his plate to the sink.

'No you don't,' I say.

'I'm Chelsea all the way through!' he says.

I look past him, out of the window, wondering whether it's naively optimistic to hope for more snow.

After a long break, September comes around once more: the tortoise has begun his long transition from summer's nuisance to winter's decorative doorstop; the boiler has undergone its traditional annual collapse; there are forty-seven messages on my office phone from robots wrongly suggesting that I am due some sort of refund, and two dozen old emails on my computer wrongly stating that certain well-known people have tweets for me; and the cat, well, I'm pretty certain I saw the cat yesterday.

More importantly, the football season is in full swing, and I am embarking on my annual attempt to engage in intelligent football conversation. I used to know nothing, but I've come so far – perhaps this is the year. I don't want my children to be taken aback by any sudden display of insight or erudition; I just want to be able to make comments that either meet with approval or go unchallenged. The new season is a chance for a fresh start, and I am brimming with misplaced optimism.

At lunchtime on Sunday I find the middle one lying on the sofa in his pyjamas. The telly is roaring ahead of an imminent kick-off.

'Who's playing who?' I say, even though I know the answer.

'Liverpool Man U,' he says.

'Oh yeah,' I say, casually. In fact I have secretly been studying the Premier League table in order to determine a Chelsea supporter's position regarding this match.

'I suppose,' I say, 'that a draw would be the best result for us.' The boy raises an eyebrow and sticks out his lower lip.

'I'd be happy with a nil-nil draw,' he says, before going on to explain the various outcomes he would prefer, due to his complex fantasy football commitments. I don't understand a word of it, but I nod anyway. My wife comes in from the kitchen to ask me to chop some stuff, which I imagine will give me time to rehearse some intelligent comments.

'Who's playing?' she says.

'Liverpool Man U,' I say, a little too quickly.

After doing the required chopping, I return to the match.

'What's happening?' I say.

'Liverpool are on fire!' the boy says. Right, I think: don't ask any more questions; just look at the screen. It's clear that someone has scored while I was away. The crowd is cheering every pass Liverpool make. A comment occurs to me. One Liverpool player passes to another. The crowd goes wild. I clear my throat.

'It's certainly easy to tell which stadium this is being played at,' I say.

'Uh-huh,' the middle one says. Anfield, I think. It's called Anfield. A silence follows.

'I mean, you can tell because of the crowd,' I say. 'At this point they're effectively cheering continued possession.' I am pleased with this. I steal a glance at the middle one. His face is a blank.

'Well, yeah,' he says. 'You can tell from the cheering, and the chants, and the shape of the stadium, and the fact

Liverpool's name comes first, and the fact that United aren't playing in red.'

'Obviously,' I say, feeling my face heat up. I think about excusing myself to go and chop more stuff, but it's too early to surrender. A lame shot from Sturridge is easily blocked; it's quite clear to me he should have passed.

'Useless,' I say. In the ripening silence that follows, I realize he must have scored the goal I missed.

# CHAPTER FOUR

One of the first aspects of fatherhood to strike me as a distinct advantage was being in possession of a ready-made companion. If there was a baby in the car with me, I realized, then technically I wasn't talking to myself. If I ever fancied company for a particular outing, I could simply commandeer a child as a sort of tiny personal assistant. Unlike dogs, children are allowed in supermarkets and on the beach. Unlike my wife, my children are not in a position to refuse.

Occasionally – not often – I harbour a desire to go see a play. The date I might choose to attend would be based on nothing more than the earliest availability of two decent and adjacent seats, but I also know it's as good a predictor as any of a random day in the future when my wife will be ill. I'm not saying she does this on purpose. She has issues with the theatre that probably affect her immune system.

By the time the date on my latest pair of tickets rolls around, my wife has already been in bed for two days. Under my domestic stewardship, the house has come to look as if it's been turned over by burglars. After struggling downstairs to give us all a hoarse bollocking, my wife slumps in a chair and looks at me.

'It's the theatre tonight, isn't it?' she says.

'Yes,' I say.

'I don't think I can go,' she says.

'I'm not going alone,' I say.

'Take him,' she says, pointing at the oldest one, who is watching TV.

'I will,' I say, defiantly.

'Take me where?' says the oldest.

'You can't be angry with me for being ill,' she says, coughing.

'I'm not angry with you,' I say. 'Can't I just be angry?'

'Oh my God,' says the oldest. 'Take me where?'

As we drive to the National Theatre, I try to explain the premise of Alan Bennett's *The Habit of Art* to the boy in a way that won't reveal the extent to which it probably isn't going to be his cup of tea.

'It's about an imagined meeting between W. H. Auden and Benjamin Britten,' I say. 'One's a poet and one's a composer.'

'But they never actually met,' he says.

'They did, but not this time,' I say. 'And it's a play within a play. And they're both gay. That's all I know about … Oh Christ. This is the wrong way. We're going over the bridge!'

'What's the point of writing about a meeting that didn't happen?'

'We're on the wrong side of the fucking river! Why did I drive?'

I have promised the boy all kinds of pre-curtain food, but by the time we get to the theatre it's too late. As the play starts, I soon stop worrying about whether or not he's enjoying it, because I'm distracted by the woman next to me. She's a head-swiveller, automatically turning in an admonishing fashion in the direction of any noise from the audience. She's like a weather vane for rustling paper and whispering, and she seems to be capable of rotating her head through 360 degrees. Her vigilance is far more distracting than any actual noise, I think.

Midway through the first half, my son starts gently riffling the pages of his programme. The woman next to me immediately turns towards the source of the noise. I want to stay his hand, but not while she's looking – I don't want to give her the satisfaction. When she looks away, it's because he's stopped. When he does it again, she looks again.

'It's great, don't you think?' I say brightly in the interval.

'There's no queue for ice cream,' the boy says. 'Give me some money.'

As the first bell rings, he returns with an ice cream for me and an enormous chocolate bar for himself.

'You can't eat that in there!' I say. 'It's foil-wrapped!'

'So?' he says.

'So, the woman next to me is a head-swiveller,' I say.

'A what?'

'She turns towards all sound. She probably can't help it, but it's—' The second bell goes, and the crowd begins to shuffle towards the doors. 'Just don't make any noise.'

About five minutes into the second half, I hear the first crinkling of foil. I can tell that the boy is trying to time the noise so it coincides with the big laughs, but he is occasionally out of sync, and each time I hear the crinkling, from the corner of my eye I also see the woman's head swivel his way.

TIM DOWLING

This is so unfair on me, I think. I just wanted to see a play. I stare straight ahead, wishing we could all just forget about the foil and concentrate on the graphic discussion of illicit gay sex on stage.

I was six, I think, when I was first allowed to go to the shops by myself, or rather in the company of my best friend at the time, who was clutching a signed note from his mother that said, 'It is OK for Bradley to buy cigarettes.'

My oldest son was also about six when I first let him go to the shops on his own, although he wasn't really on his own, because I followed him, creeping along the opposite side of the road and ducking behind parked cars. It was another two years before he could be trusted to come back with whatever it was he'd been sent out to get, but from my point of view this was a long-term project: one day I would have my own little army of minions, with three times the errand-running power that Bradley's mother could command. I would never have to go to the shops again.

Many years on, I am trying to make lunch from things we already own.

'We could have a simple spaghetti,' my wife suggests, 'with tomatoes and garlic.'

'We could,' I say, consulting the cupboard, 'if we had any tomatoes, or garlic. Or spaghetti.'

'Send one of them,' she says, indicating the array of children spread round the room.

She's right, I think. That's what they're for, after all.

'Here's some money,' I say to the oldest. 'Please go and get the following.'

'It's raining,' he says.

'The shop is fifty yards away.'

'You go then,' he says.

In recent weeks, the corner shop has been closed for renovations. The next nearest shop is only another fifty yards away, but this means negotiations have become twice as protracted.

'Go and get a tin of dog food,' I say to the youngest.

'Why me?' he shrieks, collapsing onto the floor.

'Because I found you first,' I say. 'You'll have to go down to the main road. The close shop is still shut.'

'No way,' he says. 'Too far.'

'Nonsense,' I say. 'When I was your age I walked three times as far just to get Bradley Lehan's mother some cigarettes.'

'What the hell?' he says.

'I'll go,' says the middle one.

'Thank you. Here's the money.'

'I need more than that,' he says. 'Dog food is, like, 99p.'

'No, it isn't,' I say.

'It is down there.'

'Is it?' I say. 'Well, here then. Get two tins.'

Later in the afternoon we need milk. Again, the middle one volunteers. 'How much is a big milk down there?' I ask.

'About two pounds, I think.'

Come evening I find him alone downstairs, chewing gum and watching the football scores.

'I'm sorry to do this to you,' I say. 'But the dog ate all the cat's food before you got the dog food, so now we need cat food.'

'One pound fifty,' he says, holding out a hand without looking up from the television.

'Shocking,' I say. 'Where'd you get the gum?'

'I had it,' he says.

The next morning when I come in from walking the dog, I notice a small display of price stickers affixed to the wall just inside the front door. Two of them say 61p, the price of a tin of dog food. One says £1.32, another 99p.

'Stealing is bad,' I say to the middle one later. 'But I'm more disappointed about the lying.'

He smiles a little sideways smile to indicate that for him the lying was the best part.

When we run out of milk again that night, I can't find any of my children. Finally I am forced to step into my shoes and pull on my coat. As I open the door, the middle one suddenly materializes on the stairs.

'Where are you going?' he says.

'The shop,' I say. He reaches into his pocket, pulls out a pound coin and hands it to me.

'Get me a Galaxy,' he says. 'Keep the change.'

A few days after writing about my middle son's amusing habit of stealing my money, he marches into my office waving a copy of the column over his head.

'This is all lies,' he says.

'What are you talking about?' I say.

'I didn't stick any price tags to the wall,' he says. 'I hid them under the doormat.'

'I found one stuck to the wall.'

'That wasn't me,' he says.

'You're not denying the actual theft, I notice.'

He decides – then and there, I think – that his days of running errands for me are over.

\* \* \*

The oldest one suggests a group outing: a present-buying mission to the shopping centre the day before his mother's birthday.

'Yes,' I say, trying not to sound surprised by the word 'birthday'. 'We'll leave here in forty-five minutes.'

Forty-five minutes later, all three children are gathered in the hall, ready to go. 'Are we walking or driving?' the oldest asks.

'I don't know,' I say.

'Driving,' the youngest says.

'Driving,' the middle one says.

Ten minutes later, we're at the end of our road, in the car, staring at the gridlocked intersection ahead.

'We should have walked,' the oldest says.

'Let's turn back,' the middle one says.

'We can't,' I say. 'There are thirty cars behind us. We're stuck.'

Forty minutes later, we're halfway up a ramp leading to a roundabout. There are cars ahead of us, behind us, above and below us. None of them is moving. 'You can see the mall from here,' the oldest says.

'I can still see our house,' I say. I think about sending one of the children back there, for blankets and soup.

More than an hour after setting off, we finally find ourselves wandering among the bright lights of a department store, picking up scarves and putting them back. The social anxiety I suffer in large retail environments begins to steal over me. I sweat. I am the worst possible leader of an expedition like this one.

'I have no idea what to get,' I say. 'This place is freaking me out.'

'Perfume?' the youngest says.

'Perfume,' I say, 'is a minefield. You don't want to get stuck talking to a perfume lady. Let's get out of here.'

We pass a range of beauty products. 'Overpriced moisturizer,' I say. 'That could work.'

'What is it?' the youngest says.

'Just pick two. Nothing that says "damage repair" or "age reduction".'

The woman at the counter asks if my purchase is a gift. When I say it is, she offers me a third item. I think it's meant to be complementary, but it's unclear whether it's also complimentary. I'm embarrassed about not understanding the rules, and find myself at a loss for words. She names two options, then blinks at me expectantly. I stare back.

'I don't know,' I say.

She repeats the options, a little impatiently. I feel my face warming.

'You,' I say, pointing to the middle one. 'Choose.'

'Whatever you said that wasn't lavender,' he says.

This choice, for some reason, entitles me to another choice. Again, I don't even understand the question. She tries to simplify things: 'Face, hands, eyes or hair,' she says.

'Your turn,' I say to the youngest. 'Don't think.'

'Hair,' he says. The choices keep coming, but I find there is no decision I cannot delegate.

'Washbag or box?' she asks.

'Go,' I say to the middle one.

'Box,' he says.

'Brown or green?' she says, indicating two bottles of scent, one of which will be sprayed on the tissue paper surrounding the box.

'Smell both,' I tell the oldest, 'and pick.' He chooses green.

'And finally,' the woman says, 'can I get some samples for any of you today?' I nod to the middle one. He shakes his head.

'We're good,' he says.

On the way back to the car park, as I'm subtracting time saved from time squandered, my phone rings.

'Where are you?' my wife asks.

'Out, but we're on our way back,' I say. 'We'll be, like, ten minutes.'

It's dark when we exit the car park, dark enough to see the unbroken lines of tightly packed tail-lights stretching in every direction.

In our neighbourhood, when we first moved in, there were more corner shops than corners. There was one up the road and four along the little parade. One was also a post office, and all five were also off-licences, even though there was also an off-licence.

Eventually one shop closed, as did the off-licence, as well as the second chemist and the greengrocer who once looked at me as if I had two heads because I asked for parsley. I spread my patronage pretty evenly across the remaining four shops. There have been many nights when I have visited them all in search of an ingredient none of them stocked.

A few months ago it became known that the pub was going to be turned into a Tesco Express. There were petitions against it in all the shops – I signed several – and some anti-Tesco banners were put up, but the project had about it an air of inevitability. The local anger carried an undercurrent of doubt, as if people were thinking – if not exactly shouting – that a Tesco Express might be quite handy. I tried to be fatalistic.

'It's a shame,' neighbours would say when I met them in the park.

'The first time you need double cream on a Sunday night,' I would say, 'you'll be in there.'

A week before the Tesco opening day, I am in the second shop along the parade, buying some peanuts so I will have the correct change to pay the oldest's bass teacher. The woman in front of me asks for an uncommon brand of cigarette, which is produced instantly.

'That's why I'll always come here instead of Tesco,' she says. We all laugh uncomfortably.

Two days later I am in the shop up the road, getting a newspaper. The woman ahead of me is a few pence short.

'Let me off this time,' she says to the shopkeeper, 'or else I'll go to Tesco.' We all laugh uncomfortably.

In the other shops, the customers seem jittery, as if they are buying provisions ahead of a gathering storm. When the Tesco opens, they don't know how they'll react.

I don't think I can ever enter the Tesco, if only because it's directly across the road from three of the shops. The people who run them would be able to see me coming out, my bags filled with tarragon and brie and coffee ice cream, and I would never again be able to drop by for a can of condensed milk and four AA batteries, and watch *EastEnders* while standing in the queue. On the Friday the Tesco opens, I stay away from the parade.

On Sunday morning I find myself up at 6 a.m., ready to drive the youngest one to school so he can meet a coach to watch Chelsea play Manchester City away.

'He needs a drink for his packed lunch,' my wife says. 'You'll have to stop somewhere on the way.'

'Nothing will be open,' I say. 'It's still night.'

We drive as far as the corner before I pull over, and point.

'The new Tesco is open,' I say. 'Look.'

'We could go in there,' the boy says.

'I was thinking that you could go in there, while I stay here,' I say. I hand him a fiver. He disappears into the brightly lit pub. The rest of the parade is dark and shuttered; a horrible vision of the future.

The boy returns with a four-pack of Lucozade.

'What is that?' I ask.

'Four for £1.67,' he says. 'Amazing.'

'What was it like in there?' I say.

'Pretty much like a supermarket,' he says. I start the car.

'Tell me everything,' I say.

A week later I mentioned my inclination to avoid the new Tesco Express in a newspaper column, accidentally turning a vague intention into some kind of pledge: I had put it in writing. It was never meant to be a serious boycott; I was just pissed off that the pub was no longer a pub, even though I almost never set foot in it when it was. I felt a bit guilty about that, and figured the Tesco Express deserved, at the very least, the same level of neglect. Besides, I thought, I have kids for that sort of thing.

Another Sunday, some months later: my wife is out all morning, and I've been charged with making lunch. I open the fridge, hoping to find sufficient ingredients for a meal, but I end up compiling a substantial list. Afterwards, I find the middle one lying on the sofa watching Sky Sports News.

'It's midday,' I say. 'Are you ever going to get dressed?'

'I *am* dressed,' he says.

I look him over: he's wearing a dark-green New York Jets onesie.

'Would you go to the shops dressed like that?' I say.

'Yeah,' he says.

'*Will* you go to the shops dressed like that?'

'No.'

I find the youngest one playing on the Xbox while barking a running commentary into a headset.

'Can you go to the shops for me?' I ask.

He pulls the headset to one side. 'I'm trying to kill these people,' he says.

'But I need you to go down to the Tesco Express for some—'

'You can't keep sending your children to the Tesco Express,' he says, 'just because it's against your principles.'

'I don't see why not,' I say. 'It's not against your principles.'

'I'm busy,' he says.

I have actually been in the Tesco Express a number of times since it opened. Eight times, in fact. I always leave feeling like a creature deluded and derided by vanity, partly because I've betrayed a principle for the sake of convenience, but mostly because they never have what I want anyway. I invariably promise myself that my most recent visit will be my last.

My children are clearly not in a mood to conspire. I pocket my list, pull on my coat and head down the road.

The Tesco is brightly lit and busy. I know from experience that on a Sunday it's the only place you can buy a chicken breast within walking distance, but as usual they have none of the other things on my list: no ginger, no coriander, none of the stock cubes I favour. I realize I could pick up all this stuff at the shop over the road, but then I'd have to go in there holding a Tesco bag with two chicken breasts in it.

I am furious with myself, because this has now happened to me nine times in a row and I still haven't learned my lesson.

I'm standing in front of the chiller cabinet, frowning at their three remaining chicken breasts and grunting audibly in frustration, when I realize I'm attracting stares. As I step back and sidle along the aisle, I feel two sets of eyes following me. Have I been talking to myself, or swearing under my breath?

I suddenly feel as self-conscious as if I were shopping in a New York Jets onesie.

As I turn to scrutinize the shelf behind me, a young man in his twenties steps up and touches my arm. I turn to look at him.

'Are you Tim Dowling?' he asks.

'Yes,' I say.

'I thought you said you'd never come in here.'

*The Hobbit* was the first book I ever put down. I was twelve or thirteen. Before that, I had failed to finish a book for many reasons – a lack of application; a gradual dwindling of interest; a lost library copy – but never because I'd decided, on the basis of twenty or thirty pages, that it was rubbish. Up until then, I had never really held an opinion about literature, but now I had a position: I don't read books where the swords have names. I promised myself I would never make my children read *The Hobbit*. I might even forbid it.

It is not of my own free will, therefore, that I find myself sitting in a cinema on a Saturday afternoon trying to jam 3D glasses over my regular glasses. I am here because my wife felt able to characterize my reluctance to take the youngest one to see *The Hobbit* as an example of my failure as a father, and as a man.

'You never do anything you don't want to do,' she says.

'I mostly do things I don't want to do,' I say, 'but most of those things don't last three hours.' The boy looks up at me with his big blue Gollum-eyes. I think of all the fool's errands I have dragged him on over the years, simply because I wanted company. I book tickets.

Within minutes of the film starting, I have decided that high-frame-rate 3D doesn't agree with me: there are dark, fogged spots at the edges of my vision and I find the scale confusing. Gandalf looks huge, but he's surrounded by dwarves and tiny furniture. Perhaps he's only supposed to be 5 feet 6 inches. They should put a phone box in the corner of the room, to give the viewer some perspective.

As the plot unfolds, all my old objections to the genre resurface in the form of questions. What year is this meant to be? What kind of apples are those? Which way is New York?

I look over at my son with a disapproving smirk. In his 3D glasses he looks exactly like a miniature Kim Jong-un. When I turn back, there is a woman in a huge fur coat and hat standing up two rows in front of me, blocking half the screen. Only when Gandalf speaks to her do I realize she is actually a heavily foregrounded dwarf. I close my eyes.

When we return home many hours later with the ingredients for supper, I feel as if I have been on a quest. 'Let us cook many things,' I say to the youngest one. 'And let us tell many stories, in order to allow this cheesecake sufficient time to defrost.'

'Whatever,' he says.

It's past nine when we finally sit down to eat, but we are, for a Saturday night, uncharacteristically quorate.

'How was *The Hobbit*?' my wife asks.

'It was actually OK,' the youngest one says.

'Are you kidding?' I say. 'It was *awesome*.'

'Seriously?' says the oldest one.

'It was great!' I say. 'Rocks fighting each other, people all flying on eagles everywhere.'

'Should I go see it?' the middle one asks, narrowing his eyes sceptically.

'You should go tomorrow,' I say. 'The only problem I had is that people speaking Elvish makes me drowsy. I slept through this whole, like, elf board meeting in the middle, but then, when I woke up, there were—'

'Hang on,' the middle one says. 'Are you recommending a film that you fell asleep in?'

'I fall asleep in most films,' I say. 'It's not necessarily a criticism.'

'How can they make three whole films out of such a short book?' the oldest one says.

'It's not that short,' I say.

'How would you know?' my wife says. 'You've never read *The Hobbit*.'

I turn to look at her. 'You're goddam right I haven't,' I say.

## Lessons in primatology 2

Occasionally the younger members of my family raise objections to the way they are portrayed in print, largely in an attempt to extort money from me. I can see that being described as looking 'exactly like a miniature Kim Jong-un' merely because you are wearing 3D cinema glasses could be annoying; I just don't think it's injurious enough to justify damages to the amount of ten quid. For this reason it has become temporarily necessary to disguise the identities of people appearing on these pages. This safeguard will not, I trust, distort the basic truth of what follows.

So, anyway, my life partner – we'll call him Sean – is on this fashionable new fasting diet that allows him to eat normally for five days a week, provided he consumes no more than 500 calories on each of the remaining two days. According to Sean, this strict regime has improved his energy levels, if not his mood.

At lunchtime I open the fridge, which is packed with food. I always find it curious that the discipline of eating less invariably requires the purchase of additional food; in this case foods that cannot possibly be combined to exceed 500 calories. I spy a big tub of cottage cheese. I didn't even know there was still such a thing. I thought we'd all agreed to stop producing it.

Kurt, the youngest of our adopted ex-research chimps, joins me at the open fridge door. He makes the sign for 'something to eat', then shakes his head until his ears flap audibly. His meaning is clear: there is nothing to eat.

'You're telling me,' I say, glancing towards Sean, who is sitting at the table reading the paper and eating a packet of Maltesers.

He catches my eye. 'I fasted yesterday,' he says.

'I thought it was two days a week,' I say.

'Not in a row,' he says. 'You can choose.'

'So it's a movable fast,' I say, hilariously.

A brief silence follows. Kurt turns his lips inside out, grabs a banana and leaves the room.

In truth, Sean is at a loose end – his latest ground-breaking study on primate behaviour is behind him, and funding for new research is non-existent. If Sean's considerable administrative skills cannot find an outlet in the field of primatology, they are brought to bear at home, with occasionally alarming results. Throughout the house I find scraps of paper containing lists of foodstuffs with their calorific values scribbled alongside, and calculations beneath. Innovative recipe books keep dropping through the letterbox.

On the afternoon of the next fast day, I find Sean in the sitting room flicking his finger across the screen of my iPad. Anton, our middle chimp, is watching an FA Cup match.

'What are you doing?' I say.

'Going through all your emails,' he says.

'Oh,' I say. 'Wait, what? You can't do that.'

'I think you'll find I can,' he says.

'You won't find anything,' I say. 'I have a different address for incriminating emails.'

Anton makes the sign for 'shh'.

'I'm sure you do,' Sean says, 'but I'm not looking for that. I'm just checking to see how you're engaging with the wider world.'

'And how am I doing?'

'Not too bad,' he says. 'Don't forget you have that magazine party on Tuesday.'

'Shit,' I say. 'I never RSVP'd to it.'

'I think you'll find you have,' he says.

Kurt turns off the TV in disgust and makes the sign for 'What is for supper?'

'You're on your own,' Sean says. 'I'm just having a salad.'

Kurt folds back his ears, grimaces and points at me. It's a typical example of primate humour. Roughly translated, it means: you're a salad.

# CHAPTER FIVE

During breaks in the school calendar, the drama of family life bleeds into my office hours. Children scream at each other at a time when I normally have the house to myself, and my wife is screaming at me to do something about it. I want to scream back that I am working, but in truth I am trying to buy a secondhand clarinet online and I don't want to put myself in a position where I might have to give reasons. I don't really have reasons, just a computer and a credit card.

I go downstairs and, on discovering the source of the dispute between the youngest two, offer a form of mediation.

'How about if I smash the Xbox up with a hammer?' I say. 'How would that be?'

'Fine!' the youngest one shrieks. 'Please do!'

I am momentarily thrown by this response, as I always imagine Solomon must have been when one of his petitioners agreed that, yes, half a baby each sounded about fair. I go farther downstairs, where I find the oldest, still in his pyjamas, looking askance at yet another salad.

'It's one of my fasting days,' his mother says. 'Feel free to make your own lunch.' The boy pokes at the salad, and recoils.

'It's got avocado in it,' he says, sneering. 'And seeds.'

My wife turns to glare at him. 'I was put on this earth to raise you to the age of eighteen,' she says. 'After that, you're either my friend or my foe. You choose.'

'I like the seeds,' I say.

'What are you doing down here?' my wife says. 'I thought you were working.'

'I just came to see if there was any post,' I say.

'No,' my wife says. 'It's Good Friday.' I retreat back up the stairs, muttering something about it not being a very good Friday for me.

By mid-afternoon I resort to paying the children to go away, peeling off notes so the oldest one can top up his Oyster card enough to get him south of the river, and giving the other two money to buy sweets on the condition that they spend an hour in the park.

On Saturday morning I wake to the sound of the youngest two fighting over the Xbox again. An agreed rota system has broken down, apparently because the online multiplayer experience refuses to conform to a timetable.

'What if,' I say, 'I pulled all the wires out of the Xbox and ran it under the shower? Any use?'

'I wish you would!' the youngest shouts.

Saturday is haircut day – a quarterly standing appointment wherein Kelly and Hayley, who used to work in the salon up the road, come to our kitchen to do five haircuts and half a head of lowlights for a bulk price. It takes up a whole morning, and fills the kitchen with hair. After that the middle one embarks on a twin-track project: baking a cake while pausing periodically to bad-mouth Premier League footballers on his blog. The younger one spends the afternoon watching the television and his laptop at the same time. I find it quietly infuriating that neither of them wants to go on the Xbox.

That evening the oldest one returns from south of the river.

'What are you staring at?' he says.

'You missed haircut day,' I say. 'And it shows.' Above our heads I hear chairs being knocked over. My wife pauses the television.

'They're fighting over the Xbox,' she says. 'Do something.'

I go upstairs. 'If you don't stop,' I tell them, 'I'm going to take the Xbox down to the street and run it over with the car.'

'Do it!' the youngest shrieks. 'I'm begging you!'

'Seriously,' I say, 'I don't know how to react to that.'

From time to time we find it necessary to abandon our house during breaks in the school calendar, if only in order to escape the machines that rule our lives. Some people might call this 'going on holiday', but for me that's a deceptive phrase. One might also imagine that time spent in bucolic surroundings would eventually lead to some kind of outbreak of harmony, but that is not my experience. And actually, we tend to bring a lot of our machines with us.

Eventually my wife saw fit to impose a holiday no-screens rule: a ban on the use of laptops, iPhones, tablets or handheld consoles of any kind before 6 p.m., no matter how awful the weather, for the duration of the so-called break. So what did we do instead? We played games, often of our own devising. I offer an outline of the rules to some of our perennial favourites:

*Is It Six Yet?* Three or more players. All participants gather round a clock and watch the minute hand creep forward. At any point, a player may shout, 'Is it six yet?' even when the clock clearly shows that it's 11 a.m. If the umpire feels the shouting is too frequent, he may threaten to extend play until 6.30 p.m., or even 7 p.m., although he's only making a rod for his own back, frankly.

*The Break Fast Club* A perfect game to while away the hours in rented or borrowed accommodation. On a rainy or unseasonably cold day, players form a 'club' and rampage through the house seeing how fast they can break everything. Extra points are awarded for objects of sentimental value, difficult-to-replace items, the cooker, etc.

*I Hate You!* Player One selects a younger player and charges him with performing a small task or chore – hanging up a towel, perhaps, or retrieving a shoe from the roof. Player Two's response should be affirmative but non-committal ('OK', 'I will', 'I said I will', 'I'm just about to', or some other regional variation), but he must not be put off from his present activity: sitting on the floor tearing an old issue of *FourFourTwo* into tiny strips. Player One continues to repeat the request until Player Two is moved to shout, 'I Hate You!' and run from the room. Once this portion of the game is complete, Player Two is free to take out his anger on the next youngest player. Carries on for five days, like Test cricket.

*Galley Slaves* Game for two parents. Players sit opposite one another. The first to speak issues a statement along the lines of, 'I didn't come on holiday to spend the whole time washing up.' The second player counters this with something like, 'I did the washing-up this morning while you were still in bed.' The first player then says, 'I've cooked five of the last six meals, and I'm sick of it.' The second player says, 'I feel as if I've spent the entire week sweeping up broken glass, and I think I have swine flu.' This continues until one player starts packing the car.

*What Do We Bring To The Party?* Two or more families. When all forms of recreation have been exhausted, Player One, in desperation, proposes an impromptu visit to another family who happen to be holidaying nearby. A second player, doubtful of the prospect of a warm welcome, asks, 'But what do we bring to the party?' The first player lists such delights as adult conversation, children of the same age, knowledge of the local area, etc., even though the real answer is half a bottle of Pinot Grigio and nits.

The holiday place we retreat to most often is my father-in-law's cottage in Cornwall. He's owned it for decades, since my wife was a toddler, and its rusticity is authentic and unremitting: there is no TV, or washing machine, or mains water, or mobile signal, or heating beyond two wood stoves. It is accessed by a long, steep track that makes you think twice about leaving once you're there. It's beautiful, and my children have been permitted to inflict all kinds of damage upon it over the years. But it has not always provided a backdrop to our finest moments as a family, or to mine as a father.

Although some of our happiest times have been in Cornwall, our holidays there are still catalogued in our collective memory according to what went wrong: the summer the well ran dry; the time the clutch went; the year of the chimney fire; the winter we arrived to find that mice had eaten the puzzle.

Once it rained so unforgivingly for so long that the house was left standing on a little island surrounded by raging torrents, across which we ferried children and supplies. Some of the supplies didn't make it. A visiting child, who was clearly traumatized by his stay, later drew a picture of my wife standing waist-high in churning water as shopping bags swept past her, with a balloon emerging from her mouth that said, 'MY WINE MY WINE.'

At least bad weather is exciting. It takes a rare week of unbroken sunshine to remind one that nothing nature can throw at you is as testing as a week in a cottage with three children.

On the final evening of our holiday I am policing the immediate outdoors on my wife's instructions, fishing wet socks out of hedges and picking cutlery off the lawn in the late August light. I am bone weary, and secretly glad to be heading home the next day. Actually I'm not making much of a secret of it.

The final task on my list is the retrieval of the youngest one's new Frisbee from a tree, which takes fifteen minutes of poking with the longest stick I can find. It's a ring-type

Frisbee rather than a disc-type, so it's really hung up good.

Finally I manage to flick it loose. It lands on the grass at the middle one's feet. He picks it up and throws it straight back into the tree.

'What did you do that for?' I ask.

'It was an accident,' he says, grinning.

'Well, you can get it down then,' I say, handing him my stick. But he can't get it down. He's too short, and the Frisbee is now even more entangled than it was before.

Eventually I locate a branch-trimming tool mounted on a long pole, and after twenty minutes of judicious snipping I am able to cut the Frisbee free. As soon as it hits the ground the middle one picks it up again and throws it into the woods. I turn and glare at him.

'I was throwing it to you!' he says. I lose my temper. I use language that would earn a film a certificate that would prevent him seeing it for another four years.

'You go into the woods right now,' I say. 'And don't come back without that Frisbee!'

'I'm never coming back anyway!' he screams, pushing open the gate.

'Fine!' I shout. 'Live in the woods!'

My wife emerges from the house, and unfortunately this is the only bit of my parenting she witnesses. I realize that, shorn of its context, it looks bad. In the end I have to go to help him find the stupid Frisbee, because it's almost dark.

We don't only go to Cornwall. Over the years we have experimented with taking holidays in a variety of locations. But I find going elsewhere extremely stressful, especially if

I have never been to that place before, especially if I have to take work with me, which I almost always do.

'The thing about you,' my wife says as we pack, 'is that you can work anywhere.'

My wife's view of me as an essentially portable bread-winner informs all our travel plans. That's why we're back in the car after just a few days in London, heading for a cottage in some picturesque seaside town. This final leg of the summer holidays has been booked for months, but thinking about it causes a knot to form in the pit of my stomach. It just seems like an additional week in which something could go wrong – a holiday too far.

We arrive in the seaside town and are met by friends who have rented a cottage nearby. As we unpack, I give voice to several competing anxieties, about parking, about the dog, about work.

'Relax,' says my wife.

'You have to work?' our friend says.

'Don't worry,' my wife says. 'The thing about him is he can work anywhere.'

My wife goes off to see their cottage while I stay behind to establish an internet connection so I can start work. I try every gadget in my sack of dongles and wires. Nothing works. The air here has no internet in it. I end up standing on a dresser while holding my laptop out of the bedroom window, thinking about the many different places I have travelled to in order to work from: the field in Devon where I found a faint mobile signal, the hotel lobby in Slovakia, the Turkish internet cafe, the services on the M4.

Below me, my children and the children of our friends are conducting an incredibly loud conversation, half in the cottage and half in the street, shrieking at each other through the open front door. I go downstairs to tell them to be quiet.

'This is not Naples,' I say. 'If you wish to continue to—' I stop and look at the open front door. 'Where's the dog?' I ask.

'Dunno,' the oldest one says. I step into the street. The dog never runs off – it's been standing directly behind me for the last eight years – but she's not outside and she's not inside. It's obvious to me what has happened: a whole summer of continual geographical displacement has finally taken its toll. The dog has suffered some kind of freak-out and is now charging aimlessly through an unfamiliar seaside town. This is not a good start to the working day.

I send the children in one direction and I go off in the other. After a few minutes, I realize I am more or less lost myself. Eventually I reach the crowded high street. I don't see the dog anywhere, but I immediately run into some people I know.

'Hello!' one of them says. 'You look lost.'

'I've lost my dog,' I say.

We chat for a while, but we're not really on the same wavelength. They're on holiday and I'm having a panic attack. As we talk, a car drives by with someone else I know in it. He waves at me.

As I walk along I begin to think that everyone looks familiar. Across the street a door opens and a woman I vaguely recognize steps out. Most people have sunglasses on, so I can't tell whether or not I should say hello. What kind of town is this? I think. Has the whole of Shepherd's

Bush decamped here in order to experience substandard WiFi provision? What's relaxing about that?

I find it too stressful to remain on the high street – what if I meet someone whose name I can't remember? – so I duck down a quiet little lane to my left. Up ahead I see the dog coming towards me. We stop and stare at each other with sad, freaked-out eyes.

'Where have you been?' I say. 'Who have you seen?'

We sometimes go to America during the holidays, but then I'm not really on holiday, because I'm home. Once I enter the family house in Connecticut, I'm more son than father, and more brother than husband.

It is the week of my father's ninetieth birthday, and my entire family is gathering under one roof for the celebration. The little boathouse over the road has been hired for Saturday evening and sixty people have been invited, but when we arrive on the Tuesday before, very little else has been achieved.

At the morning pre-party briefing, before my brother and sister go to work on Wednesday, several decisions are made and unmade, and I am given a list of things to buy. At the Thursday morning briefing, our previous decisions are reconsidered and I am admonished for my failure to purchase certain items. Party planning is not our strong suit.

There is another problem: the boathouse lies in the potential path of Hurricane Irene, whose arrival may or may not coincide with the party. Hundred-mile-an-hour winds are forecast, along with a ten-foot storm surge, widespread flooding and power outages. In the shops, people are panic-buying bottled water, generators and torch batteries. I am panic-buying cocktail napkins.

At lunchtime, my brother emails my sister and me spreadsheets labelled Headcount, Timeline, Menu, Bar and Supplies. My sister's reply says simply, 'Nerd alert'. I can't even open the spreadsheets. In the afternoon, I panic-buy cheese and olives from shops stripped bare of essentials, and then take my wife to drop off some panic dry-cleaning. In the car we listen to reports of closed highways, suspended train services and the hurricane's northward progress. We consider cancelling the party, then decide not to, and then decide to decide later.

On Friday, my father's actual birthday, the guy in charge of the boathouse makes the decision for us: he cancels our booking – apparently they need to fill the boathouse with boats. We call off the party and schedule a smaller emergency celebration – family only – for that night. I attempt to break the news to my father, but I'm not certain he has his hearing aids in. 'The boathouse thing is cancelled,' I say.

He picks up the newspaper and sees the date on the front page. 'Today's my birthday?' he says.

'Yes,' I say.

He shakes his head. 'I could've had a free coffee,' he says.

My brother and I spend the afternoon shopping for party food, starting at the fish shop.

'No one's panic-buying lobster today, I see,' my brother says to the proprietor.

'Not really,' the man says.

'We'll take ten,' my brother says.

'Is this a good idea?' I say.

'He's ninety,' my brother says.

Elsewhere, it is impossible to buy water, candles and most kinds of soft fruit. We call my wife and sisters, who are busy getting their toenails panic-painted, and have an argument about cake. By the time we get back, my Aunt Gladys is already there, expecting food. We finally manage to get supper on the table at 10.30 p.m., after panic-drinking much of the alcohol bought for the original party.

On Saturday, I take my wife to pick up her panic dry-cleaning, but the dry-cleaner's is shut because of the hurricane, so we panic-buy some cupcakes instead. Later, at about the time the first party would have started, I find myself at a loose end. There is nothing to panic-do. I've already lashed the canoe to the back deck. I decide to make an early start on my column, because of the hurricane. I find a quiet place to work and write more or less to this point, when the phone rings. There are nine people in the house, so I'm hoping someone else will pick it up, but no one does. Reluctantly, I answer. 'Hello?' I say.

'This is the mayor,' says a voice.

'OK,' I say. The voice, it turns out, is a recorded message from the mayor. He tells me I need to evacuate immediately.

I go to the living room, where my wife is sitting with my sisters.

'That was the mayor,' I tell them. 'He says we should evacuate.'

'I think perhaps we should,' my wife says. There is a brief, uncomfortable silence.

'It'll be fine,' I say.

'These trees will crush us in the night,' she says, looking out of the window at the giant oak hanging over the roof.

'We can sleep downstairs,' I say.

'I want to go to the emergency shelter,' my wife says.

The idea of sleeping in the building where I went to high school puts me in mind of an old, recurring nightmare.

'That's crazy,' I say. 'The storm won't even hit till lunchtime.'

'I want to go,' she says.

'I think you're overreacting.'

'I think you're being a bad parent,' she says.

I need time to parse this dilemma. I wander into the room where the youngest one and my Bulgarian brother-in-law are watching hurricane news.

'It's scary,' my brother-in-law says. 'I keep thinking I'm going to die.'

'It'll be fine,' I say. But in the face of the media hype and the mayor's personal evacuation order, my insouciance is beginning to seem both hollow and irresponsible. But because I'm home with my father and my brother, I'm struggling with a competing conviction, simple and irreducible: the Dowlings don't evacuate.

In the end, my wife and I compromise: I will take her to stay with my Aunt Gladys, along with two of the children, one of my sisters and half the wine, then return to ride out the storm with the oldest one. It doesn't seem a terribly elegant ethical solution – more like a hasty division of assets – but at least we're agreed.

As we wait for the lift at my aunt's apartment block, an elderly man approaches. Our pile of blankets and rations seems to anger him. 'This is all bullshit!' he shouts. 'They're talking about hundred-mile-an-hour winds! There aren't going to be hundred-mile-an-hour winds!' I keep hoping the lift doors will open, but the lift has been turned off for safety reasons.

When I wake up the next morning, the cable television and the internet are both down. We do have a radio, but it gets only one station. Reports of Irene's progress come in snatches between songs by Hall & Oates.

At 11 a.m., the leading edge of the storm arrives. The trees churn alarmingly; the front yard becomes littered with branches. Water creeps up the driveway from the flooded road. Suddenly my father bolts out of the front door.

'Where's he going?' I say. We find him in the basement, up to his knees in water, trying to plug in his electric pump.

An hour later, the worst of the storm has passed, the pump is running and the water in the road is still waist-high. I look at my brother.

'What do we do now?' I say.

'We untie the canoe,' he says.

'Can I come?' the oldest one says. I pause to consider my moral obligation to exercise extreme caution.

'Let's go,' I say.

We launch the canoe in the drive and set off, with the boy sitting in the middle taking photos on my phone. Up ahead, a fallen tree hangs on taut power lines, creating a canopy over the flooded street.

'I don't think we should go under that,' I say.

'It's not like we have a choice,' my brother says as the current sharpens. We shoot straight through the middle. On the other side we meet a flotilla – several kayaks, a couple of dinghies, even a small sailing boat – milling about at the intersection in front of the pizza parlour.

'Don't tell your mother about this,' I say to the oldest one, even though I know the pictures will be all over Facebook by morning.

The hurricane has passed, and so has summer. All we have to do is get to the airport. Historically, this is a fraught time of missed flights, car accidents, arguments over the meaning of foreign road signs, freak weather and lost documents. That's why I've left two hours for the journey from my father's house to JFK, even though on a good day it takes forty minutes. I know this isn't a good day: it's Friday, the start of Labor Day weekend in America. To own a car and not be on the road today would be sort of unpatriotic.

We hit congestion just after we get on the main highway north, but this was predicted, and it dissipates after a few miles. I'm pleased to see I have just under a quarter of a tank of petrol: it's my aim to leave the hire company almost none of the fuel they made me buy off them.

'This car is incredibly efficient,' I say. 'I've hardly put any petrol in it while we've been here.'

'That's amazing,' says my wife, who is doing her best to find me interesting during this tense interval.

Overall the mood in the car is surprisingly calm. We're already almost halfway there, we've used up only thirty minutes of our two-hour window, and I still have an eighth of a tank of petrol.

Traffic suddenly slows to a crawl. 'This is worrying,' my wife says after fifteen minutes.

'Not really,' I say. 'It's to be expected, with everyone converging on the bridge. We've got plenty of time, and ...' I glance at the petrol needle, which shows I have a shade over a sixteenth of a tank, although the true figure might be best expressed in thirty-seconds. I turn on the traffic report. There are, it says, major delays on the approach to the Whitestone bridge.

'Are we going to miss the plane?' the youngest one asks.

'No,' I say, lowering my voice, 'but I'm a tiny bit worried about petrol.'

'Why don't you stop there?' my wife says, indicating a service station up ahead. Traffic begins to thin out as we approach it.

'It's not that bad,' I say, sailing by the exit. I realize my mistake almost immediately. Arriving late is no longer the worst-case scenario.

The tailback at the bridge is huge. Flashing signs estimate the journey time to JFK at forty-five minutes. The toll booths that accept cash are at either edge of the road, and when the left-hand queue stagnates, I cross eight lanes of angry traffic to try my luck on the other side. This manoeuvre is not compatible with my personality, and I find myself making a distressing keening sound.

'Stop it,' my wife says, 'you're going to have a heart attack.' At this moment, a coronary event sounds like a welcome deliverance.

Traffic on the bridge proceeds by inches. As we rise towards the middle of the span, the petrol gauge dips below zero, and so do I. 'Oh God!' I scream. 'We're going to run out of petrol in the middle of the Whitestone fucking bridge!' It is a startling failure of leadership.

'I don't understand why you didn't get petrol back there,' my wife says.

'I should have!' I shriek. 'But I didn't!'

'Why don't we get off and get petrol now?' the oldest says.

'There is no off!' I shout. It's true. Even after we cross the bridge, every subsequent exit leads to some other choked parkway twisting up and over us. There's no telling which roads lead to petrol and which to ruin. I press on, inch by inch, teeth clenched, knuckles white, eyes wild.

Six miles from the airport, I crack, pull off into an unfamiliar part of Queens, buy some unleaded, and get slightly lost retracing the route. We arrive at the airport exactly two hours after we set off. Perfect timing, I think. But I don't say that, or anything else, for a long while afterward.

# CHAPTER SIX

My father was a dentist. I know how easy it is to ignore a lecture about the evils of sugar, even when it's being given by a parent who is at that moment also drilling out a cavity in one of your upper molars on his day off, in his tennis whites and in a hurry, because he has a court booked for eleven.

Back then neither of us could have imagined how perverse society's approach to eating would become: for the sake of convenience, we basically live on poison. I'm well aware of the importance of instilling in my children a healthier attitude towards food than I actually possess myself, but I also suspect that The Way We Eat Now, dysfunctional as it is, may be scant preparation for the ingestion practices of the future, when sugar is all that's left. For all I know, our present approach to eating and meal-times may be just the training my kids need. Fortunately it doesn't matter if I get it wrong, because I'm their father: they don't listen to me.

My son and I are lying on a couch apiece, watching the penultimate instalment of the *MasterChef* final. I love

*MasterChef:* I can't think of any show on television that asks less of me.

The dog walks into the room looking guilty. It's not a facial expression as much as a certain postural cast, a way of lowering and extending the neck.

'What have you done?' I say.

'When?' my son says.

'Not you. I'm talking to the dog.'

One of the *MasterChef* contestants is learning to make a tear-shaped dessert garnish out of glucose syrup and chocolate. Suddenly the dog coughs up something that resembles a large, freshly peeled potato. Before I can recoil in horror, she devours it again, whole, and walks out of the room.

'Oh my God,' I say. 'Did you see that?'

'You just lift it up with a spoon until the sugar hardens,' my son says. 'It's not that big a deal.'

'Not that. The dog just ...'

For a brief moment I doubt what I have witnessed with my own eyes: a family pet regurgitating one of its own organs, and then resorbing it. I follow the dog into the kitchen.

There I find a scene that more or less explains everything. There is a child in pyjamas standing on a chair in front of an open cupboard, in the act of easing a biscuit tin off the top shelf. Behind him on the table is an empty plate, and on the floor a distressed wrapper that once contained a large block of supermarket cheddar. It is immediately obvious that the cheese's distinctive, hard-edged, trapeziform profile must have taken on a more potato-like shape as a consequence of its two trips through the dog. Three trips now, I think. And then I think: three trips so far.

'Where's the cheese?' the child says, turning round.

'You left it on the table and now the dog's had it,' I say. 'Why are you even eating cheese at this hour? You're supposed to be in bed.'

'I didn't do anything!' he shrieks, and storms off.

I lock the dog in the garden, as both punishment and precaution. Over the next hour, I allow myself to slip into a quiet fury, broken only occasionally by the sound of the dog thrusting its head through the catflap and whining. This episode is emblematic of our familial disregard for food, I think: children and animals helping themselves to handfuls of whatever they fancy all day long. Things must change.

The next morning there is a shredded, empty cat-food box lying on the kitchen floor. This latest crime smacks of something beyond the cat's tiresome persistence or the dog's opportunism. It appears to be the product of an unholy collaboration. It occurs to me that I may have neglected to feed either of the animals the day before, but I decide not to say anything.

That night my wife makes supper: chilli from a posh grocer's, heated up. I turn the telly to face the table, so we can watch the last instalment of the *MasterChef* final.

'There's no cheese,' my wife says. 'Sorry.'

Thinking about the cheese again puts the absurdity of the situation into perspective. We are eating a ready-meal while watching people train in three-star Michelin restaurants. 'I hate to say it,' I say, 'but I think we need to start having supper with the children. As a family.'

'Don't be mad,' my wife says. 'Not in the week.'

'They eat nothing at mealtimes,' I say, 'and they help themselves to rubbish all day. I'm worried we're not setting a very good example.'

'I do hope,' my wife says, pointing at the telly with her fork, 'that you're not going to talk all the way through this.'

My wife and I never did officially set a starting date for eating with the children – family-style, if you will. But as time went on their supper hour got later, ours got earlier, and the two began to collide. A separate sitting for adults began to seem like a poor deployment of resources – it was reserved for special occasions when we wanted to eat exotic foods the children would not countenance. Finally even that phase came to an end: if we cared to experiment with food, the children became unwilling subjects.

One night I come downstairs to find a large, rarely used pot on the hob and a cookery book next to the sink open to an unfamiliar, unstained page. Three boys lope warily into the room behind me.

'What is this?' says the youngest one, staring at the plate that's been handed to him.

'It's poison,' says my wife. 'Sit down.'

'Not there,' I say. 'I sit there.'

'What the hell,' says the youngest.

'Don't speak like that,' says my wife.

'I always sit here,' I say.

'Where am I supposed to sit?' says the youngest.

'Just sit anywhere,' says the middle one. 'It doesn't matter.'

'Shut up,' says the youngest.

'You shut up.'

'Stop bickering,' says my wife, before turning her attention to the oldest one. 'And you – hold your fork like a normal human being.'

'This is pleasant,' I say. 'Who would like to tell us something about their day?'

'Today,' says the middle one, conducting the air with his knife, 'I built a little bird house.'

'In your soul?' I say. He stares at me with blank eyes.

'No, in DT.'

'I'm finished,' says the youngest.

'No, you're not,' says my wife. 'Eat some more.'

'Oh my God!' he shrieks, collapsing dramatically.

'In certain highfalutin' circles,' I tell him, 'it's considered impolite to rest your forehead on the table.'

'Yes, sit up,' says my wife.

'But I'm done!' he shouts, jumping to his feet. As a social occasion, the family supper still has a few procedural details to be negotiated.

'Right, then you put your plate in the dishwasher,' says my wife. 'And then you come back and sit down and chat nicely.'

'What?' he says. 'Why?'

'It's a punishment for eating too fast,' I say.

'No,' says my wife, 'it's not.'

'No, exactly,' I say. 'It's about being together as a family.' He slouches to the bin, then the dishwasher, before returning dejectedly to his seat. A long silence follows.

'I had an interesting tweet from a reader today,' I say.

'Oh good,' says my wife, 'your father's going to talk about himself.'

'It said – I'm paraphrasing – "How do you get paid to write this shit?"'

'Swearing at the table,' says the youngest one.

'And I wrote back, "By BACS."'

There is another long silence.

'I'm finished,' says the middle one.

'Which is a sort of automated clearing system, so it was—'

'Me, too,' says the oldest, leaping from his chair.

'I give up,' says my wife, refilling her glass and standing up. 'Everyone has to help clear the table.'

I am the only one who remains seated. 'Don't take the wine,' I say.

'Leave the pots and pans for your father,' says my wife as she heads for the sitting room. 'He can wash up.'

'That's like a punishment for eating too slowly,' I say.

'Yes,' she says. 'It is.'

My wife has other culinary punishments, particularly if she feels I haven't been pulling my weight in the kitchen. On Fridays, for example, she sometimes comes home with a load of random ingredients and presents them to me as a meal-in-waiting, as if I were a contestant on *Ready Steady Cook*.

'What am I supposed to do with this?' I say, peering into the bag.

'That's for you to decide,' she says. I never, ever, do this to her.

As suppertime approaches, I am overtaken by a failure of imagination. My wife, sensing this, steps in. I find her in the kitchen doing something experimental with leeks.

'I thought,' she says, 'you could make this.' She points to the open page of a cookery book, to a recipe for potato rösti. The ingredients are few, the instructions relatively straightforward. My only objection at this point is to the word 'rösti'.

'Yeah, OK,' I say.

I peel and parboil several potatoes, and leave them to cool while I watch the news and think up better names for the side dish I am about to add to my repertoire. 'Who wants potato pucks?' I will say. My children will remain silent, wondering where to look.

When the potatoes reach room temperature, I grate them, add salt and pepper, and form them into shallow rounds, disregarding, as the book instructs, their unwillingness to hold their shape at this stage.

I transfer the flattened blobs to the frying pan. As I watch them cook, I decide that the effort expended has been insufficiently transformative – I am staring at something that is transparently still just a bunch of potatoes. Why bother? It occurs to me that existence is futile.

After a few minutes I attempt to turn over the rösti using that kitchen tool for which the English have no good word, having already assigned the term 'spatula' to a large and virtually useless knife. As I lift the first one, the cooked portion sticks to the pan, exposing the raw grated potato beneath. It happens with all four of them, on both sides. This could carry on, I think, until I'm left with nothing but a pan that needs washing up. I slap one of the rösti with the flat of the kitchen tool, deforming it.

'I hate you,' I say.

'How's it going?' says my wife, who has somehow materialized behind me.

'They're a failure,' I say. 'I've failed.'

'They look all right,' she says.

'No,' I say, 'they don't.'

She leaves the room. As the rösti continue to disintegrate under my care, I experience a rising anger. I've yet to look up the word 'rösti', so I don't know the term *Röstigraben* – literally, 'rösti ditch' – referring to the cultural faultline between German-speaking Switzerland, where they eat rösti, and the French-speaking part, where they don't. But I am coincidentally thinking about tossing my rösti into a ditch, pan and all.

In my frustration, I whack the worktop with the tool. This is incredibly satisfying. I throw the tool at the wall, which is less satisfying. I consider throwing the pan, but the kitchen has been recently painted. My indecision tips me over the edge. You, I tell myself, are worthless. I go upstairs and lie curled on the bed, allowing a bottomless *Röstigraben* of despair to open beneath me.

It's not an auspicious start to a breakdown, I think, but my wife and children will excuse that once they realize the extent of my collapse. When they find me here, a hollow-eyed, gibbering wreck, they won't ask what happened to the rösti.

Except that, after a few minutes, I start to feel better. My heart stops pounding; my breathing slows. Instead of contemplating my own unravelling, I begin to wonder if I can get back downstairs before anyone notices I'm gone, and make rice.

Clearly it wasn't really about the rösti at all, but just the same I make a solemn vow never to eat one again.

Eventually children reach an age when they wish to develop their own dysfunctional relationship with food, through cooking. I never encouraged this, but that didn't stop it happening.

'Dad,' the middle one says, 'can I make something?'

I look up from the sofa to see him holding a cookbook under each arm. 'It's nine o'clock at night,' I say, 'so it's not really—'

'It won't take long,' he says.

'What is it you want to make?'

'Sushi.'

'No. We don't have any—'

'Fine,' he says. 'Croissants, then.'

'Shall we just see what's on the … Oh, look – *Wife Swap USA!*'

The lesson he drew from this exchange was: don't ask. The next time he decides to cook, I don't hear about it until he arrives at a crisis.

'Dad!' he shrieks. 'I need help!' I go downstairs to find the kitchen fogged in airborne flour. The cupboards are flecked with chocolate and the floor crunches under my bare feet.

'What happened in here?' I say.

He points to a bowl on the worktop. 'I used double the amount of sugar in the recipe,' he said.

'Why?' I say.

'It was a mistake! And it's already mixed up with the eggs!'

'Then just double the amount of everything else,' I say.

'We don't have enough of anything else,' he says. The mathematical nature of the dilemma appeals to me. I grab a pencil.

'How much sugar did you put in?'

'Er, 350 grams,' he says.

'How many eggs are in there?'

'Five whole, two yolks,' he says. I put the pencil down.

* * *

It was inevitable, given their closeness in age, that the cooking bug would eventually infect his brother.

'Dad, I need money,' the youngest says one morning, shaking me awake. It's a Sunday. The clock says 7.30.

'What for?' I say.

'Marshmallows,' he says. Some time later I detect a strange, sickly-sweet burning smell. I get out of bed and go downstairs. Once again, the kitchen looks as if it has been the subject of an attack – a warning left by angry mobsters. The youngest is in the sitting room watching *Wife Swap USA*.

'Want to try?' he says, holding up what looks like a rough-hewn chunk of MDF with one gnawed-off corner.

'Bit early for me. What is it?'

'A Rice Krispies square,' he says.

'Ah,' I say. 'Why does it look like that?'

'They only had pink marshmallows,' he says. 'And we were out of Rice Krispies, so I used Shreddies.'

'This is my house and you will follow my rules,' says a man with a Tennessee drawl. The boy turns back to the telly and resumes gnawing.

'What's it taste like?' I ask.

'Bit weird, actually,' he says.

By this stage the middle one has grown bored with cooking, but the hiatus lasts a matter of months. The sudden restoration of his enthusiasm stems directly from a fresh glut of cookery shows: *Celebrity MasterChef*, *The Great British Bake Off*, Lorraine Pascale. He watches them all. Over the course of two weeks printed recipes from the relevant websites chug out of Darth Vader's head while I'm working.

'What's that one for?' I say when he comes up to retrieve his pages.

'Lemon posset,' he says.

'Ugh,' I say.

'It's good,' he says.

'Sorry,' I say. 'It's just that word: "posset".'

'I might make something else as well,' he says.

When I go down to the kitchen, there are stacked bowls on the table and pools of yellow stuff dripping from the worktop. The boy is at the hob, staring into a saucepan full of apples.

'They're still hard,' he says.

'How small did it say to cut them up?'

'I just guessed,' he says.

'What does Mary Berry of *The Great British Bake Off* say?' I ask.

'"You're fired."'

'No. Mary Berry says, "Follow the effing recipe."'

'Mary Berry doesn't swear.'

'If Mary Berry saw this kitchen, Mary Berry would—'

'Gotta go,' he says, handing me his wooden spoon. His renewed passion for cooking has unfortunately coincided with the imminent closing of the football transfer window, obliging him to divide his time between the kitchen and Sky Sports News.

My wife walks in. 'Look at this mess,' she says. 'It's your fault for making him do two puddings.'

'I'm not making him do anything,' I say.

'He's doing the whole apple thing because you said posset was disgusting.'

'It's just the word,' I say. 'It means "baby sick".'

'Are they still hard?' the boy shouts from the other room.

I go back up to my office. An hour later, a recipe for salmon saltimbocca drops into the printer tray, but no one comes to get it. When I eventually drift back downstairs, the kitchen is empty but the oven is on. I find the middle one in the sitting room watching *The Great British Bake Off*.

'They sit down on the floor to watch their ovens,' I say.

'I know,' he says. 'Weird.'

'Whereas you watch them watching their ovens, leaving your oven on its own.'

'Shit!' he says. 'The apple things!' He runs into the kitchen. Mary Berry accuses someone of having a soggy bottom.

The boy comes back in.

'They're a bit burnt, but it's cool,' he says. He puts *The Great British Bake Off* on pause to cook the saltimbocca. On my wife's instructions, I hover behind him, offering advice.

'I think you're supposed to put the sage on the inside before you wrap them,' I say.

'I didn't actually read the recipe,' he says.

'I know,' I say. 'But I did.'

'You're supposed to be encouraging,' my wife says.

'But firm, like Mary Berry,' I say.

Supper isn't ready until some time after nine, but the salmon, thanks in no small part to my timely intervention, is an unexpected triumph.

'Who wants posset?' the boy says.

'I will try some,' I say. He puts a tall glass of yellow stuff in front of me. Under everyone's eye, I take a cautious mouthful.

'It doesn't taste at all like I thought it would,' I say. 'How much baby sick did you put in?'

'A surprisingly huge amount,' he says. 'And you still have your apple thing.' He slides some form of turnover towards me.

'I'm not sure I can manage that.'

'You have to,' my wife says. 'He made it specially.'

They all go off to watch the rest of *The Great British Bake Off*, leaving me alone with my second pudding. The edges of the pastry are slightly singed, but the apples are still quite hard.

# CHAPTER SEVEN

When I was young, my father came home from the office at 6.30 p.m. every day. On winter evenings, he would stick his cold hands down the backs of our collars when he arrived, and we would squeal with delight. I never got to do this with my children; I'm a freelance writer. I rarely leave the house during the day, and my hands are always slightly clammy.

Instead, it was my children who came home in the evenings, with loosened ties and free newspapers tucked under their arms. I would greet them excitedly at the door, while they tried to edge past me. If I asked them about their day, they would mumble something about the people in charge being idiots. They knew better than to ask me about my day. They didn't need to hear another monologue about someone calling me a prick on Twitter.

At first I was unsure what sort of example I was setting for them. I always knew exactly what being a dentist was, because my dad was my dentist. A typical Saturday outing with my father would consist of a trip to the lab that made dentures for him.

What I do for a living doesn't look like anything, or rather, it looks like a man who is sitting in front of a computer, but not really using it. They also knew I went to the park sometimes, to walk the dog. Perhaps, I used to think, they tell people their father is a dog-walker.

The path at the front of the park is being relaid, and my main objective for the afternoon is to stop the dog wading into six inches of wet cement for the second time in the same day. Having failed, it is my revised aim to prevent the dog from getting wet cement all over the furniture. Here I do not succeed either. I also have an article to finish. In this, too, I am failing.

At about 4.30 p.m., the doorbell goes. It is the older two, back from school. I hear them giggling over the entryphone.

'What's funny?' I ask.

'That's like Dad,' says one of them quietly. They start laughing again.

'What's like me?' I say.

'Let us in!' they shout.

I push the button and go downstairs, where they're shedding coats and shoes on the floor, still laughing.

'What is like me that's funny?' I say.

'We had to watch this video in PHSE,' the middle one says.

'What is PHSE?' I say.

'Personal health and social education,' the older one says.

'It was called being "Being Different",' the middle one says, 'and there was this kid in it who said, "I'm different because my mum goes out to work and my dad stays home all day."' They stare up at me with idiotic grins on their faces.

'We're Different,' the older one says, gurning. The middle one laughs.

'You're more than different,' I say. 'Frankly, I think you're both a little bit special.'

I return to my office and fail to write an article over the course of the next hour. At 5.45 p.m. I give up and go downstairs. My wife is reading the newspaper while the three boys watch television.

'Well, look who it is,' she says sarcastically. 'Look, children. It's your father.'

I don't know what she means by this. It's not me that's been anywhere. I sit on the couch. The children are watching one of those programmes made up of mobile phone footage of people falling over. It epitomizes all my overruled objections to the recently installed satellite dish. 'This is the worst programme I've ever seen in my life,' I say.

'It is rubbish,' the oldest says.

'I've seen this one before, anyway,' I say. Feeling guilty, I stand up to leave the room.

'Where do you think you're going?' my wife says.

'I still have a bit of work to finish,' I say.

'How convenient,' she says.

I go upstairs and fail to write an article some more. A while later I hear my wife on the landing below me. 'Why is there dried mud all over the bed?' she shouts.

'It's—' I stop there, suddenly realizing it would be a tactical mistake to point out that it's actually dried cement.

'Yes,' my wife says, 'I'm not surprised you're lost for words.'

Some day, I think, I shall have a job where I work far away from home, and then they'll see what's Different. Who will walk the dog three times a day? Who will take delivery of the neighbours' packages? Who will let the electrician in, or put pans under leaks when it rains? Who will tell the Jehovah's Witnesses that, yes, of course they can leave a copy of the *Watchtower* if they like? Who will read the *Watchtower* in its entirety?

Then I realize that this day will never come, because I have become unfit to work in an office surrounded by other people. I lack the basic interactive skills. Perhaps it's because I never took a class called PHSE, and so have no Social Education.

My computer screen goes black because I have not touched the keyboard in half an hour. I stare at my gaunt reflection in the darkened glass, and my reflection stares back at me. Oh well, I think. At least you have your Personal Health.

As my children get older I feel less like a stay-at-home dad and more like a neglected pet. Sometimes it makes me want to chew up something they own. I would like to be able to demonstrate some kind of professional competence for their benefit, but I can see that knowing when to use a semicolon is never going to inspire much in the way of admiration.

My dentist is explaining what he's just done to me. 'I've built up the side of the tooth,' he says.

I nod. My manner is sober, collegiate: because my father was a dentist, I like to give the impression of expertise. Go ahead, I want to say, use the jargon. But my face is too numb to talk.

At home that afternoon we watch the tennis on television while conducting a family conversation of unsurpassed inanity.

'Why don't clouds cast shadows?' the middle one asks.

'Because they're not under the sun,' my wife says.

'Clouds do cast shadows,' the oldest one says. 'Big ones.'

'Oh yeah,' the middle one says.

'Stop asking stupid questions,' my wife says.

'Who's stupid?' says the middle one. 'You just said clouds were above the sun.'

'No I didn't.'

'Every cloud casts a shadow somewhere,' I say. My contribution feels weighty, like an aphorism, until I instantly think of a contrary example: a cloud under a cloud.

'Shut up about clouds,' my wife says.

'You're a cloud,' the middle one says.

The youngest one appears. 'Watha thcore?' he says.

'Why are you talking like that?' I ask.

'My bwaithe,' he says.

'What?'

'I told him not to fiddle with his brace,' my wife says. 'But he did, and now he's broken it. Again.'

'I thaid thorry,' he says.

'Let's have a look,' I say, moving the lamp closer. 'Open, please. Wider.' I peer in, and describe my findings. 'A section of the apparatus, which runs from molar to molar across his palate, has come loose.'

'I've seen it,' my wife says. 'I'm taking him on Monday.'

'He can't live like this until then,' I say. 'Can he?'

'It's the weekend,' my wife says. 'What can I do?'

'Is there an emergency number?'

'I'm sure there is. Call it.' It occurs to me that an emergency appointment may incur an emergency fee.

'You call it,' I say.

'You're a cloud,' the middle one says.

We sit down to supper, but the boy cannot, will not, eat. His exasperation casts a cloudy shadow over the meal. I think about my father, rising from the dinner table on Friday nights to treat patients who had swallowed their partial dentures, and experience a sudden realization.

'I can fix this,' I say.

'Uh-oh,' the oldest one says.

'Come with me,' I say.

The youngest one follows me into the sitting room and, at my bidding, lies with his head on the arm of the couch. I shine a camping torch into his mouth and tug gently on the loose component. It gets looser still, but remains fixed to the wire running through the upper brace. The arrangement is familiar: I used to wear braces, and fiddle with them.

'Wait here,' I say. I run to the tool cupboard.

'Whath thath?' he says when I return.

'Wire cutters,' I say. 'They're rusty, but sharp.' He is eerily calm as I stick the point in his mouth and clamp it round the wire. I find his trust touching, if a little unnerving.

'Here we go,' I say. 'Tongue out of the way?'

'Yeth.'

'Good. Don't move.' I squeeze. There is a loud *snip* as the component comes away in my hand.

'Whoa,' he says.

'How does that feel?' I ask.

'Great,' he says. 'Thanks.' He returns to the kitchen and sits down. I follow him in a minute later, clutching my trusty, rusty wire cutters.

'Next,' I say.

\* \* \*

My wife tells me she's ordered a new shed. Our old shed, with its rotted roof and holed floor, is filled with the kind of stuff you don't mind getting wet – mostly cracked pots, shredded plastic sheeting and leaves. I have long maintained that getting by with a useless shed for so many years proves we don't really need a shed.

'It's nothing to do with you,' she says. 'I'm paying someone to put it up, and to take away the old one.'

'Good,' I say.

By sunset the new shed is in place and my wife is so pleased that I begin to regret my unhelpfulness. The next morning, she is gone by the time I get up.

'Where have you been?' I ask when she returns.

'I bought a potting bench and some shelves for the shed,' she says, holding out her keys. 'They're in the back of the car.'

The potting bench doesn't look like a bench. It looks like a bunch of wood wrapped in plastic with a picture of a bench stuck on the front. Before I can stop her, my wife has opened the plastic, letting the loose timber clatter to the ground.

'Shall I get you the drill?' she says.

It takes four and a half hours of false starts and free-form swearing to put the bench together. Frankly, I'm a little disappointed it's gone so well.

'That wasn't so hard, was it?' my wife says.

'Yes, it was,' I say.

'What about the shelves?'

'Tomorrow.'

The next morning I rise early to find the youngest one watching TV alone. I open the back door and see the constituent parts of the shelving unit lying on the patio. I stare at them for a bit. Then I turn back towards the television.

'Come and have a look at this,' I say to the youngest one. 'It's like a puzzle.'

He stands over the pile, a length of stainless steel edging in one hand and the pictorial instructions in the other.

'You bolt these together first, for the sides,' he says. 'Then you add the shelves, two bolts for each corner.'

'Are you sure?' I say. 'Because I think you might need to—'

'I'm sure,' he says. 'Get me a wrench.'

'OK, but first we should just—'

'It's fine,' he says. 'I can do it by myself.'

The sun comes out. I make coffee and pull a chair towards the open garden door, just out of sight, where I can listen to the birds singing and the youngest one muttering under his breath as he crouches over the instructions, wholly absorbed in my chore. It is the nicest morning in my memory. With any luck, I think, he'll be finished by the time my wife comes downstairs.

I hear the bright ring of a steel shelf tipping over and hitting the ground, the unpleasant squeak of metal on metal and the sound of a tiny nut rolling across a paving slab.

'For the love of fuck,' says the boy, quietly.

# CHAPTER EIGHT

Constance is not one of my children, but her parents were among the first of our friends to have a baby, long before my wife and I were even married, so we have known her since she was born. They lived a few doors down from us in those days, and sometimes we would babysit. As a child Constance had a bewildering stillness about her that slightly freaked us out, but that was a long time ago now.

Constance has come to stay with us for a few days. She has stayed with us before, so we know what to expect, but it's always still a little surprising.

Overnight, I have forgotten she's in the house, but I remember as soon as I wake up because I find her perched on the end of my bed, talking to my wife about a dress.

'You need to help me pick one,' says Constance.

'Not right this minute I don't,' my wife says.

'Why is she in here?' I say, my voice a thin croak.

'Tim!' shrieks Constance. 'How can you say that?'

'Can you make her go away?' I say to my wife.

'Tim,' says Constance, 'why have you got a beard?'

'I don't know,' I say. Overnight, I had also forgotten I have a beard, but I feel it now, like a small itchy jumper tied to my face.

'It makes you look so much older,' she says.

'What time is it?' I say. 'Why is this happening?'

'You should shave it off,' she says, leaving the room. My wife and I look at each other in silence.

'I'm glad we only have boys,' I say.

'So am I,' my wife says. From the other side of the door I hear Constance shriek, '*How can you say that?*'

I get up and go downstairs. I can tell Constance has got hold of my wife's phone, because as I'm making coffee I receive a text from my wife that says, 'I love u so much I am nothing without you lets renew our wedding vows.' At about this time our youngest son, at football practice, receives a text that reads: 'You are my favourite child.' The middle one gets: 'I always wished you were a girl.'

When I return to my room, Constance is there, sitting cross-legged on the bed, reading the newspaper.

'Tim,' she says, 'it's so weird that you're American.'

'Is it?' I say. She turns the page.

'Do you like being American?'

'Yes,' I say.

'Are you proud to be an American?'

'Yes. Not really. Don't know. Yes ... Actually, I refuse to answer.'

'Whatever,' says Constance.

'But as an American, I require a rather surprising amount of personal space. In fact, I would like it if ...' She turns towards the door.

'*You need to help me with this fucking dress!*' she shrieks.

From elsewhere, my wife shouts back. I grab my clothes and go in search of a safe place to put them on.

Half an hour later my wife comes in from walking the dogs, double-thumbing her phone as she enters.

'What are you doing?' I say.

'Apologizing,' she says. 'She texted random names in my address book, with things like, "You are my best friend." A lot of people were alarmed.' I can hear Constance in the other room, talking to the youngest one, who has just returned from football and is trying to watch TV.

'Do you love me?' she says.

'No,' he says.

'Are you sure?' she says.

'How long is she staying?' I say.

'Don't worry,' says my wife. 'We're going away.' I'd forgotten we were leaving Constance in the house on her own for the night. We depart hastily and without listing any particular rules for her to follow, other than the one we established the last time she came to stay, which is Under No Circumstances Should The Cops Be Here When We Get Back. Over the weekend we receive only two texts, one that says, 'When does the hot water come on?' and one that says, 'Where is the wine?' so I have every reason to hope, as we turn the final corner for home, that this time they won't be.

Constance is actually one of four sisters, and when they all come for lunch things get loud. It is not at all the kind of loudness I am used to, which normally consists of the crack of a football repeatedly hitting venetian blinds, punctuated by swearing. This noise of Constance and her sisters is much closer to what I imagine it's like to work in that room at the airport where they quarantine all the exotic birds people try to smuggle into the UK: one squawk setting all the others off, the cacophony rising in both volume and pitch until your ears overload. My sons are cowed into silence by it.

My wife loves it, and makes herself heard by bellowing over the top. I do my best to join in, but my concentration fails and I find myself staring into the middle distance. My wife waves a hand in front of my face.

'Are you ever going to say anything?' she shrieks. Looking around the kitchen, I realize I can actually feel the noise against my eyebrows.

'When?' I say.

'What?' she shouts.

I am sent out to get more wine. It's amazingly quiet outside. On the way back I wave to a neighbour.

'I hope that's not wine in that bag!' she says. I think she has read in my column that I am not drinking, which was true last week. But this is this week.

'No,' I say, resting the bag against my thigh to stop the bottles clinking together.

The noise hits me as soon as I open the door. It contains notes of both delight and panic, as if people were bravely trying to conduct a cocktail party during a train derailment. They've just discovered that the youngest one is missing.

'Where is he?' my wife shouts.

'I don't know,' I say. 'He's probably hiding.'

'Find him!' shouts Constance.

'Bring him here!' shouts her sister. 'We love him!'

I find him in his room, sitting at his desk.

'Your presence is requested,' I say. 'Come downstairs.'

'I'm doing my homework,' he says. 'So no.'

'I can't really go back down there without you, so … wait – you're what?'

'Doing my homework,' he says. I notice he has a textbook open and is making marks on a worksheet. He's also watching a movie on a laptop and talking to someone on the phone, but it's still an odd sight.

'Is he coming?' my wife shouts as I refill my glass.

'No,' I say. 'He says he's doing his homework.'

'He's not getting away with that,' she says. She goes to the foot of the stairs and calls him, deploying the special, chainsaw-edged howl she reserves for communicating over distance.

As lunch gets under way the conversation divides into three, and becomes ear-splitting. Suddenly the sister at the far end pounds the table with her fist until everyone turns her way. She introduces a single topic: religious tolerance.

'And,' she yells, snatching up a set of keys, 'you can't speak unless you're holding these!'

'Bollocks!' my wife shouts.

'You don't have the keys!' everyone else shouts.

'Then give me the keys!' my wife shouts. The keys sail through the air and smash into the fridge.

'I think we should use a banana,' I say. 'Someone's gonna lose an eye.'

'You don't have the keys!' everyone shouts. My wife retrieves the keys and holds them over her head.

'I disagree with everything!' she shouts.

'There are bananas in the bowl just there,' I say. The keys fly past me back towards the sister on the end. She grabs them.

'Why have we never thought of this before?' she shouts.

# CHAPTER NINE

I can ski. I am, actually, a pretty competent skier, having started at a young age. I stopped for a while, but I started again when I had children, because I wanted them to ski too. It was a difficult decision, because being able to ski in the UK marks you out as a very particular kind of middle-class undesirable: privileged, foolhardy, environmentally indifferent. It's not something one automatically wishes to saddle one's children with, but I wanted my children to learn so I would have people to ski with who weren't as good as me. It's unlikely my children will ever be markedly better skiers than I am; I just can't afford it.

My wife does not ski, and hates skiing, but she also thought it was important for the children to learn, because it was something we could all do together without her. This is her idea of the perfect winter holiday: the kind where she doesn't come.

She usually overcomes my grave reservations about such an arrangement by organizing everything, and because she is not coming on the trip herself, she is never afraid to economize. We go where we're sent.

*   *   *

In order for our Slovenian ski holiday to be a success it must end soon, and without further incident. Within an hour of arriving on the slopes I had one of the children throwing off his skis and shrieking at me in front of the long queue for the button lift, which was stalled because another of my children was lying in a tangled heap in its path. The third one, mercifully, was missing. At that point I walked over to the ski school hut and booked them all two hours of expensive private tuition.

The day would have ended happily, had we not been tempted by the prospect of night skiing. This meant lugging all the skis back to the hotel, then back to the slopes, and then back to the hotel. On the last journey I was carrying three sets of skis and two sets of poles. My sense of humour had long since deserted me.

The rest of the trip was a delicate balance of highs and lows, of laughter at dinner, bickering by the heated pool and tears on the slopes. I kept my wife updated by phone.

'They're trashing the hotel room, and we've lost a glove,' I said.

'But it's fun? You're having fun?' she said.

'The middle one had a meltdown at the top of the chair lift and refused to move,' I said. 'Then we had a forty-five-minute argument about where to have lunch. Then I screamed at them about the glove.'

'So is it a disaster or is it fun?'

'It's fun,' I said flatly. 'We're having fun.'

On the last day everyone is skiing happily and confidently, but if the holiday is to be a qualified success, I must get them off the slopes and to the airport without anything else going wrong. One of them, however, has made a Slovenian acquaintance, and is refusing to quit.

'I'm skiing with my friend,' he says. 'I don't need you.'

'We're leaving!' screams his brother. 'Now!'

'I don't care,' he says. I am too tired to argue with him.

'One more run,' I say. But one turns into two, and then three. By the time we get to the ski hire place, the youngest two are in a protracted argument about who is stupider. I pull off their skis and clatter down the steps to the hire shop with as much as I can carry. An English couple are asking the man behind the counter speculative questions about hiring equipment. I run back up the steps to get more skis. The youngest two are still arguing.

'Be quiet!' I yell. 'We're in a hurry. Pick up this stuff and follow me.'

Back downstairs the English couple are trying on boots. I start to take mine off, feeling for my shoes under the bench.

There is a sudden burst of swearing and slapping from outside, followed by the sharp ring of metal on metal. The youngest two enter the shop in mid-fight. They are actually hitting each other with ski poles – ski poles that I am tantalizingly close to returning undamaged. Their two little faces are purple with fury. The man behind the counter shakes his head and looks at the English man.

'They're not mine,' says the English man, with a disapproving snort.

I try to pitch myself forward in time to the point at which I will find this funny, but I can't get past the moment a few seconds hence when I will have to shake my head ruefully and say, 'They're mine.'

\* \* \*

I am skiing down a long, straight run, approximately 2,500 metres above sea level. Behind me I can once again hear the sound of swearing and ski poles clanging in anger. We've come a long way from that hire shop in Slovenia. Three years and several expensive lessons later, my children have graduated to fighting while travelling downhill at twenty miles an hour. Despite my determination to keep well ahead of them, they eventually draw up either side of me.

'He's being a total idiot,' the middle one says. 'He just hit me with his pole for no reason.'

'It was an accident,' the youngest one says.

'That is such a lie,' the middle one says.

'Oh. My. God,' the youngest says.

'You shouldn't fight while you're skiing,' I say. 'It's not safe.'

'I'm never skiing with him again,' the middle one says.

'As far as I'm concerned,' I say, 'no one is ever skiing with anyone again.'

Later I get into a rather public argument with the youngest one because I won't let him ski alone. It's a battle I've already fought and lost – he's been skiing alone for an hour and a half – but I've suffered a late pang of conscience over my lack of supervision. From his point of view, this sudden reversal is monstrously unfair. He makes this point in a manner that leaves me wondering how many people in the immediate vicinity understand English.

'Don't call me that,' I say.

'Why not? That's what you're being like.'

'You're coming with me,' I say. 'And that's that.' After this exchange he refuses to speak for the whole of the long ride up the chair lift. I stare into the mist, feeling slightly guilty for being glad of the peace and quiet. Somewhere below us I can hear a father shouting at his child, and I think: jerk.

At the top of the mountain the weather has turned nasty: a hard wind is driving heavy snow across the piste, rendering its contours invisible. In these conditions, it seems steeper than I remember.

'This is terrible,' shouts the boy above the wind's rip. 'I hate you, Dad!' I pick my way down the slope until his outline fades, but as soon as I stop it begins to sharpen up again, making tight little turns in my direction.

'I can't believe you forced me to come up here!' he shrieks. 'I'm freezing! This completely sucks!' A year ago I would have had to coax him down one turn at a time using a combination of promises, soothing words and terrible threats. I probably would have had to carry his skis part of the way. I notice, however, that his skiing has really come along over the course of the week; all I have to do is retreat to the limit of the audible range of his abuse, and let him catch me up.

A few hundred metres down, everything changes again. The wind dies and the sun comes out. With my hat off, I can hear birds singing. From out of the mist I see the boy racing towards me, arms out, coat flapping. As he passes he turns to look at me with cold blue eyes.

'You don't have to wait for me,' he says.

Italy: my wife has described this Easter late booking to me as a triumph of cost-cutting on her part. This would account for the fact that our destination is a six-hour drive from the airport where we landed, and why our two-room apartment comes equipped with very little. This is how I find myself shopping for bare essentials early on Easter morning. A few shops are open, but none is the kind that will sell me a washing-up brush.

Despite my wife's budget-consciousness-by-proxy, skiing is still an inherently expensive pastime. Every time someone shows me a bill I have to resist the urge to let my mouth hang open. By the time we hit the slopes I am thinking only of the hard times ahead. By the time our first lunch is paid for I feel obliged to conceal from my children the fact that we are ruined.

'After that lunch we don't really need supper,' I say to the older two that afternoon. 'Just some basics – milk, wine, a washing-up brush.' Eventually we find an open shop.

'Here,' the middle one says, pulling scouring sponges from a shelf.

'That's a packet of three,' I say. 'We just need one cheap brush.'

'Don't even pretend you don't want these,' he says.

When we get back to the apartment my wife calls.

'How's it going?' she says.

'There has been some challenging behaviour,' I say. 'And some unforeseen expense.' I put a brave face on everything. Later we receive a Skype call on the laptop from my family in America, who appear to be spending Easter drinking champagne in the sunshine while my nephew burbles contentedly in his car seat.

'We're in Italy,' I say. 'Skiing.'

'Don't break anything,' my sister says.

'We always do,' I say. It's only later I realize she meant bones, whereas I was thinking of cups, chairs and light fittings.

After a quiet meal of chocolate eggs, we turn on the television and pass the time revoicing an Italian-dubbed episode of *NCIS* back into English, taking charge of a character apiece. I play the sombre head agent trying to solve the mystery of a corpse found in the woods while his colleagues giggle, swear profusely and spontaneously declare their desire to have sex with one another.

'Enough!' I say finally. 'It is time to wash up. There is a scouring sponge for each of you, just like the royal family have.'

'I need to charge my phone first,' the middle one says.

'I need to charge my iPod,' the youngest says.

'It's my turn to charge,' the oldest says.

'I am charging the laptop,' I say, snatching our only European adaptor from the youngest one's hand, 'because I have to get up before dawn and write my column, and I'm worried about it.'

'What's it gonna be about?' the middle one says.

'I don't know,' I say. 'That's why I'm worried.' I push the adaptor into the socket upside down. There is a loud sparking sound, and all the power in the apartment goes dead. We stand in the pitch-black for a moment, in silence.

'Why don't you write about this?' the middle one says. Something like a guitar string snaps in my head.

'This?' I shriek. 'I can't write about this! I can't write about anything, because there's no fucking electricity!'

Somewhere behind me I can hear the youngest one trying to suppress a fit of laughter. There, in the dark, I promise God that if he gives me a better idea for a column by morning I will never go skiing again.

God does not give me a better idea. I end up writing about my ski experience to that point, and when it appears online a few days later someone appends a comment which reads,

'I don't like to be a pedant, but it's not funny if it's not true. Actually in this case it wouldn't be funny if it were true. There is no up or down to plugs used in Italy. The type used in the UK has an up and down, but they are not symmetrical, so it would be impossible to insert it wrongly.' Reading it over, I find it difficult to believe he doesn't like being a pedant.*

As the Gatwick Express pulls into Victoria station, I count bags and coats for what I hope is the last time.

'It was a good holiday,' I say to the oldest. 'Let us never speak of it again.'

'OK,' he says.

My wife will not tolerate this pact of silence. She created the perfect recipe for six days of mayhem, and she wants a full debriefing.

'Was it fun?' she asks as we pile through the door.

'Yeah, it was good,' the youngest says.

'Your father looks as if he's had some kind of near-death experience.'

'I've been given another chance,' I say. 'That's the important thing.'

---

* I don't normally respond to comments – I don't really want people to know I read them – but the accusation of falsehood angered me. I did a lot of research before I replied: 'The socket in question was a grounded universal "schuko" type, which appears to be designed to accept common C- and F-type European plugs, as well as the weird and lesser known Italian L-type, with the extra prong in the middle. And while it's true that you can stick any Italian plug in it either way round, there does seem to be a definite right and wrong way to insert a British-to-European adaptor. I hope this explains why the incident was funny.'

Platitudes do not interest my wife. She requires only details. 'What was the very first thing to go wrong?' she asks.

I tell her that shortly after leaving I discovered I didn't have the credit card on which the flights, hire car and apartment had been booked. This, it turns out, didn't matter, at least until an Italian cashpoint refused to give me any money on any of my remaining cards. This, it turns out, didn't matter either – another cashpoint was less rigorous in its assessment of my finances – but after each scare it took longer for the colour to return to my cheeks.

'What about the skiing?' my wife asks.

I describe what it's like to be suspended above the Alps on a stalled chairlift while two of your fellow passengers are trying to have a fistfight.

She smiles at this, but wants more. 'So you ski all day. Then what?'

'Then Dad would select an errand friend,' the middle one says.

Each evening I forced one of my children to accompany me on a shopping excursion, to carry stuff, pass the time and bear witness to any small humiliations. Apart from hello, goodbye and thank you, my Italian extends to just one phrase, *Lo stesso*, which means 'the same'. It serves well enough in restaurants, but in shops you sometimes have to linger until another customer appears.

'What kind of meat is that?' the oldest said as we left a butcher shop during his turn as my errand friend.

'I don't know,' I said, 'but the lady before me in the queue wanted it, so it must be OK.'

My wife isn't interested in this stuff. 'But what,' she asks, 'was the worst moment of the whole week?'

The children stop to think for a minute. 'Probably when Dad skied into the pit,' the middle one says.

'I suppose that was the only full-squad, four-man meltdown,' I say.

'The pit?' my wife says.

'It was more of a trough,' I say.

I explain that on day four we awoke to find it snowing heavily. Conditions on the slopes were challenging, and we were already heading back for an early lunch when visibility dropped to zero. The other skiers vanished. We picked our way slowly downhill in a line. Unable to see my feet, I skied off the trail into a dip, and the children followed me. Against my advice, they all kicked off their skis in order to climb out; in the knee-deep, new-fallen snow, nobody could get them back on. I started out using calm and encouraging words, but towards the end I may have suggested, in raised tones, that we were all going to die on the spot.

'But the next day the snow was really good,' the youngest says.

'So you'd go back there?' my wife says.

'I don't think anyone's saying that,' I say.

The Austrian expedition is one of those isolated occasions when my wife decides to come skiing with us. She doesn't join in, but when it comes to accommodation we at least benefit from her higher standards.

On the day before our flight I wake to find my wife in the early stages of packing, making neat piles of winter clothes on the bed. Because my wife does not ski, none of the stuff in the piles is hers: she takes a largely curatorial interest in the collection, storing it in an inaccessible cupboard, lending it out occasionally and adding to it when necessary.

'For once, I think they have everything they need,' she says, proudly.

I have a strong desire to go on the sort of holiday where I lie in a bed all day and all night, occasionally glancing at the spine of a book before rolling over and going back to sleep. Ideally, I would take this holiday in my own bed. I realize that what I really want is not a holiday, but a life-sapping mystery virus. It occurs to me that I might already have one. It would certainly explain a lot. With great reluctance, I get dressed.

'You'd better check to make sure everything's here,' says my wife, before leaving the room. I look over the piles. She is right: it's an amazingly comprehensive collection of gloves, coats, fleeces and socks. There's only one thing missing. I go downstairs.

'Where's my hat?' I say.

'What hat?' says my wife.

'My new hat, that I just got,' I say.

'I don't know what hat you mean,' she says.

'It used to be there,' I say, pointing in the general direction of the hallway.

'It's blue, and it has an R on it.'

'I've never seen a hat like that,' she says. This infuriates me, but it also makes me doubt the colour of the hat. And the R.

'There is such a hat,' I say.

'It might have got left in the cupboard, but I doubt it,' she says.

'Where's the ladder?' I say.

'In the garden,' she says.

I find the middle one lying on the sofa in front of the television.

'When was the last time you grabbed a random hat on your way out the door?' I say.

'I don't know what you're talking about,' he says.

'Was it blue?'

'I don't really wear hats,' he says.

'Let me put it this way,' I say, 'did you take my hat?'

'What hat?' he says.

'Am I going to find my hat in your room?' I say.

'No!'

I make the same inquiries of the youngest, peppering him with questions while rifling his drawers. At some point – about the point when I find myself dragging the ladder up to the inaccessible cupboard on the landing – I realize that this isn't really about the hat. Never mind, I tell myself: we're making it about the hat.

The inaccessible cupboard is bare. Peering into its recesses, I see nothing but four tiny buckled shoes, one pair slightly smaller than the other. Standing there with my head in a dark cupboard and my toes on the top step of a ladder, staring at the strangely formal footwear of toddlers past, I have an overwhelming sense of life being both fleeting and precarious. It's a moment I'm certain I will revisit in dark times to come.

Twenty minutes later I am stomping down the stairs, heels ringing on each tread, filled with a renewed sense of righteous anger. I intercept the middle one on his passage from the sitting room to the kitchen, and hold my hat up in front of his face so he can see the R.

'Where did I find this?' I say.

'Dunno,' he says.

'IN YOUR ROOM!' I shriek.

He smiles broadly, with the uncomplicated delight of a toddler stepping on his first snail.

'Oh dear,' says my wife, from halfway up the stairs.

We arrive in Austria to find it snowing hard. One does not expect an April skiing holiday to be plagued by a surfeit of snow, but this is what happens. Snow blows in sideways all day on Tuesday, and all night. In the morning, it's still snowing. Large sections of the mountain are closed due to high winds, the risk of avalanche and too much snow.

By lunchtime on Thursday, my children have had enough of the adverse conditions; I cannot persuade them to ski even one more run, despite my determination that they experience misery commensurate with the money I've spent. 'Fine,' I say. 'I'll ski by myself.'

The middle one raises a pole in acknowledgement as he slides off, his form dissolving into the churning whiteness. The youngest one is already gone.

At the top of the lift, all the signs and trail markers have been coated with driven snow. The wind is a deafening howl, but I experience it as a kind of silence – my children have been bickering and swearing at each other all morning, and now they're not here. I take a deep breath and set off in the general direction of down.

I try to keep to the middle of the trail, veering left occasionally to counteract the effect of the wind. After a while, I stop to regain my bearings, but it's a bad idea: the skiers below me instantly disappear. My immediate surroundings are an undifferentiated blankness and I am utterly alone. I am also, I realize, still moving. Suddenly, I feel air under my skis. At this point, the only organ sending useful information to my brain is my inner ear, and it's indicating that I am no longer vertical.

The ground smashes into me from a wholly unexpected direction. My shoulder makes an unpleasant crunching sound and my ears ring inside my helmet. I sit up and wipe the snow from my goggles, but the scene before me doesn't change. After a moment, I hear the faint scrape of skis somewhere above my head. A four-year-old without poles materializes, turns neatly round me and vanishes.

When I get back to the hotel my wife is lying on the bed and reading a book.

'How was it?' she asks.

'I'm broken,' I say.

'Don't be such a baby,' my wife says. 'You're on holiday.'

On Friday, everything changes: the wind drops, the sun appears, the sky turns a hard blue. We're on holiday with friends, but we haven't skied with them yet because their kids are smaller and have lessons all day. Today, in spite of our wide range of abilities, we ski as a pack. The conditions are perfect, and the pain in my shoulder has faded. My children are surprisingly patient with the younger ones, shouting encouragement and scooping them up when they fall.

'That was the best skiing ever!' my friend says at the end of the day. 'And your kids are completely charming!' I shrug.

'I guess they can be when they want to be,' I say.

'Seriously,' he says. 'They're a credit to you.' We're sitting outside at a crowded bar, the sun is just setting and I have a second beer before me. Perhaps I really am on holiday, I think. Or maybe I died in that fall. Whichever.

The youngest one finishes his hot chocolate and gets up to go back to the hotel. He turns to my friend. 'Thank you very much for everything,' he says. 'I had a great time, all the usual formalities, etcetera.'

'He's so polite!' says my friend.

The middle one puts down his drink, slides off his stool and looks at both of us. 'See you on the flipside, mother-fuckers,' he says.

Eventually we moved our annual Cornish week to October half-term, when you can always make the argument that the terrible weather is at least seasonal. The main drawback is that I usually have quite a bit of work to do in late October, but I've finally come to like bringing work with me on holiday; it makes me feel important, and it allows me to cry off any bits of the holiday I think I might not enjoy. In any case there isn't much else to do in Cornwall in late October.

That changed with the advent of the cheap wetsuit. Suddenly my oldest son was keen to get in the water, even in October, even in the rain. This, I decide, is one of those bits of the holiday I might not enjoy.

In the morning, after everyone goes to the beach, I retire to my temporary office – a patch of nettles on top of a hill where I can get a faint mobile signal – and make calls while sheep stare at me. In the afternoon everyone returns, sandy and tired.

'Breakfast still not quite cleared away, I see,' my wife says. The oldest one and his friend drift though the door.

'How was surfing school?' I ask.

'They were both really good,' my wife says. 'They're going back tomorrow.'

'You should come,' the oldest one says.

'If I finish work,' I say, 'I'll come and watch for a bit.'

'No, you need to surf,' he says. I consider this challenge carefully. I don't like to think of myself as someone who is too old to learn to surf, unless it will get me out of surfing.

'I have nothing to prove,' I say.

'Yes, you do,' he says.

The next day my wife drives the three of us to the beach. I lean my forehead against the passenger window, looking up at the leaden sky.

'What's wrong with you?' my wife asks.

'My back hurts,' I say.

'They do loads of stretching first,' the oldest one says.

'Wait,' my wife says. 'Is Dad actually doing surfing?'

'Yeah,' the oldest says.

'Is that why he's being so unpleasant?'

'Probably.'

The large crowd around the surf-school van gives me hope that they won't have room for me, but they do. There are twenty-nine of us in all, with my son and I representing opposite ends of the spectrum of ability. After struggling into damp wetsuits, we end up in different groups.

It looks as if there are a few men my age in the beginners' group, but this is only because I tend to forget what my age looks like when I'm away from a mirror. In fact they're probably ten years younger than I am, and in any case they are there to accompany their kids, who are my true classmates.

For an hour we practise the proper way of paddling ahead of a wave, getting on the board and maintaining the correct surfing posture, all while standing still on the sand. Mothers circle the class taking pictures of their kids.

Finally we are herded into the surf. The waves aren't big, but the currents are unpredictable and the available space is teeming with learners. I abandon several attempts to catch a wave for lack of room. When I do find a little clear water, it takes me so long to run through the procedure – paddle, grip rail, raise torso, kneel, jump – that by the time I get to my feet I'm on the sand again. As I turn around, the oldest one rides a wave into shore and hops off in front of me.

'Have you got up yet?' he asks.

'Not really,' I say. 'It's too crowded.'

'Come out with us,' he says, pointing to the distant circle of experienced surfers sitting on their boards.

'I'm only allowed in up to my waist,' I say. He shakes his head and paddles off.

I stalk back out, cold and exhausted, and wait for a wave I can call my own. Finally it comes. I assume a kneeling position and scramble awkwardly into a crouch. The board is surprisingly steady beneath me. I stand a bit taller. I'm actually surfing, I think. A small girl – perhaps nine – crosses my path, board held sideways. I try to turn, but I don't know how to turn. I pitch backward off the board. The wave crashes on top of me, rolling me over and driving water and sand into my ears. I sit up, spluttering and disoriented, to find the girl looking down at me and smiling.

'Well done!' she says.

We're in France, spending a week with Constance's mother, and Constance, and Constance's sisters. We've been here before, and I am practised at adjusting to the dramatic shifts in volume. In the mornings, when everyone under twenty-five is asleep, it's so quiet that I can hear a horse sneeze a mile away. After supper, with ten people seated around the kitchen table, the conversation becomes deafening.

'I think we should play a game!' my wife shouts.

'We've been playing a game for twenty minutes!' the middle one shouts. 'Pay attention!'

The game we have chosen is meant to be simple enough for everyone to grasp, but we've aborted the first round three times because of technical infractions, mostly committed by a single party.

'Wait, what am I?' my wife says, not for the first time.

'Have you looked at your card?' the middle one asks. His tone is familiar: patience edged with exasperation.

'Yes,' she says.

'Ace means you're a werewolf,' he says. 'Face card: you're a villager. A two means you're the seer. D'you get?'

My wife stares at him for a moment. 'I have an ace,' she says.

'Oh my God!' he screams. 'Don't fucking tell me your card!'

'Stop being unkind to your mother!' Constance shrieks. 'I love her!'

'Yes, let's all be nice,' Constance's mother says.

'Shut up, Mum,' Constance says.

Round one is declared null and void again, and the cards are redealt. The game is elaborate enough to require a neutral moderator: the oldest one, the only person in the room fully conversant with its intricacies. 'Night falls on the village,' he says. I close my eyes, and immediately experience the mild distress of not knowing where my wine glass is.

'This is fun,' my wife says.

'Mum, shut your eyes,' the oldest one says.

'Sorry,' she says.

'Will the werewolves make themselves known,' the oldest says, 'and decide who they wish to kill.'

A short silence follows; outside, a dry wind whistles through a field of stubble.

'I love this game,' Constance's sister says.

'Dawn breaks,' the oldest one says, 'and the lifeless body of Constance is discovered at the bottom of the village well.'

'What?' Constance says. 'That is so unfair.'

'Now the villagers must decide who to lynch,' the oldest says. 'Who would like to begin?'

'Am I alive?' my wife says.

'Yes!' the middle one shouts. 'Open your eyes!'

The youngest one raises his hand. 'Should we do, like, a mercy killing?' he says, pointing to his mother. 'To put her out of her misery?'

'How can you be so cruel to your own mother?' Constance shouts.

'I'd definitely vote for that,' the middle one says, putting his hand over his head.

'Oh dear,' Constance's mother says.

'Am I the seer?' my wife says.

'You are so not the seer,' the middle one says.

'Any more votes to kill Mum?' the oldest asks.

All eyes turn to me. I realize I haven't spoken for half an hour.

'On the one hand,' I say, 'her failure to understand the game means she can't cheat.'

'I'm not speaking to you,' my wife says.

'On the other,' I say, raising my arm, 'yes, I vote kill.' My wife's bottom lip juts forward theatrically.

'OK,' the oldest says. 'Mum dies, night falls.' With those words, an innocent villager – one who never learned to play by the rules – is unceremoniously dispatched.

'I can't believe you just did that!' Constance shouts. I want to explain that I acted not out of cruelty, or even impatience. But I say nothing, because I can't tell anyone my real reason: I did it because I am the werewolf.

As the years go by, our half-term holiday in Cornwall gets shortened – usually by work commitments at one end and the children's social obligations at the other – but we mostly find that the annual autumnal excursion is enhanced by abbreviation: we are no longer used to doing everything together as a family, and four rainy days seems more than sufficient. On the upside, the dogs are allowed on the beach. Sometimes I think it's really just a holiday for the dogs.

'I can't feel my legs,' the youngest says from the back seat, his eyes just visible above the bag on his lap.

'Only two more hours,' I say.

Even though we are down a child, we have packed the car with more stuff than ever; one whole bag is devoted to electronic distractions and their associated wiring. We may set off with the idea of walking along the beach with the dogs, but we invariably pack with an eye towards holing up.

It is dark when we arrive, but everything in the house is in order: the electricity comes on, the pump springs to life. The children sit in front of the fire with laptops obscuring their faces, while the dogs run in and out of the door, coming back a little muddier each time.

In the morning, we make the traditional trip into town to buy all the various things we've forgotten to bring: a dog lead, a phone charger, back-up wine. That night, the four of us play poker for three hours, using walnuts for chips, like imprudent squirrels.

On the second day, the rain arrives and settles in. For a time it rains almost as hard as it did in the year of 'MY WINE MY WINE'. We go to the beach and stand huddled, with our hands in our pockets, while the dogs gambol around at the water's edge. The old dog struggles to keep up as we pick our way back over the rocks and I find myself trying to lead it along a less arduous route. 'This way,' I say, but the dog is too deaf to hear.

On the fourth day, the sun finally shows itself. My wife prefers to pack up alone, so the rest of us make our traditional last-day pilgrimage across the fields to the nearest village. The sweetshop at the end of the walk is not as incentivizing for a fifteen- and sixteen-year-old as it once was, but at least the dogs are excited.

At the edge of the woods, we come to a freshly refurbished stile: the gap where animals might slip under has been sealed off. There is no way the old dog will get over it.

'We'll have to lift,' I say.

It's not a simple operation; the old dog is heavy and strongly objects to being picked up. It has to be passed from me to the middle one, each of us positioned on either side of the stile, while it tries to wriggle free. I think about how much harder it will be on the way back, when the dog knows what's coming.

The field on the other side is steep and muddy, and the old dog's footing falters. Halfway up, it tips over and gets stuck, eyes rolling like a panicked horse.

'I'm not sure this dog is going to make it,' I say, pulling its back legs free.

'I vote we go back,' the youngest says.

'We're already halfway,' the middle one says.

'Let's just rest here for a minute,' I say, sitting down on some damp grass.

I recall carrying both these children, one in each arm, across this field, while the dog zipped back and forth between us and the gate at the top eight times. I realize this is probably our last walk to the sweetshop together, unless the last one was the last one.

'What are we doing?' the middle one asks.

'I don't know,' I say.

Coming home on the M5, we pull over at a motorway services – Cullompton, I think – to air the dogs, use the loos and get some petrol. I feel a profound sense of dislocation when I see the prices on the pumps: how long have I been away?

The shop is quiet when I go in. I spend a few idle moments staring at the magazine rack – it's the first time I've been alone in nearly a week – and then I get a bottle of water and some Quavers for my wife. It is only as I approach the counter that I notice the till is being manned by a vampire.

I stop, turn and pretend I'm suddenly very interested in the road atlases. When I steal a second glance, I see that he is a Victorian-style vampire, with a wide-brimmed top hat, a velvet coat and a richly embroidered foulard knotted at his throat. He's also a terribly plausible vampire: his eyes are sunken pits, his ivory skin is tightly stretched over the sharp contours of his skull and blood runs from both corners of his mouth.

It occurs to me that it is Halloween. Then it occurs to me that it isn't Halloween – not yet. I'm annoyed at being obliged to interact with a man dressed as a vampire a full two days ahead of schedule. Or have they moved the date forward for some reason? When did this happen? How long *have* I been away?

I realize that when I go to pay, I should probably say something jolly by way of acknowledging the effort he's made, but I'm tired, my back hurts and I don't feel like joining in. I long for the sort of briskly efficient, slightly lemon-lipped transaction one normally associates with motorway petrol stations. The presence of a few more people might help to dilute the awkwardness of the situation, but there are no other staff on duty, and I'm the only customer. I wish I'd forced one of my children to come in with me.

I glance up again. The vampire appears tired and distracted. Maybe his manager made him put on the costume. He's probably been in it for hours – the heavy, ill-fitting coat, the lanky black wig that is possibly attached to the hat. Dozens of people will have already come up to him and said things like, 'Hey, what time are you due back in your coffin?' and he will have had had to smile as if it's the first time he's heard it. He may have started his shift in high spirits, but by now the indignity is likely beginning to grate.

Then again, it's hard to tell what's going on in his mind, because he's dressed as a vampire. Is he cross, or just undead? I look out at the car, sensing my wife's impatience. She will be wanting her Quavers.

It is not until I am face to face with the vampire that I decide not to allude to his condition in any way. It's none of my business. I put my purchases down on the counter.

'Just these and the petrol, please,' I say. His eyes, shining out from their heavily blackened sockets, are both unfathomably sad and coldly evil. They seem to bore into mine.

'Which pump is it?' he says.

'Number four,' I say, concentrating on sliding my card into the machine. When I look back up at the vampire, I am again transfixed. His face, pale as parchment, betrays no emotion – it's actually a little terrifying. His dark lips part, revealing blood-stained fangs.

'Do you need a VAT receipt?' he asks.

'No,' I say. 'I'm fine.'

On my way out another man walks into the shop. As he approaches the counter, I pause at the door to listen.

'You're looking well,' he says.

'I had a late one last night,' the vampire says.

If going on holiday with young children is stressful, going on holiday without older children is profoundly unsettling. Only when they've reached the age when they're old enough to stay home alone do you realize it would have been safer to leave toddlers in charge of your house.

This is exactly what I'm thinking as the middle one describes some sort of new YouTube challenge, something to do with ingesting a Cornetto as quickly as possible.

'So what do you do?' I say. 'Poke it down your throat, point first?'

'No,' he says. 'That would kill you.'

'Perhaps I've misunderstood the challenge,' I say.

I'm distracted because my wife and I are about to go away on a second honeymoon, to Italy. Up until now we've never left our children alone for more than a single night. Even when we do that, we don't tell them we're leaving until the car is running, to prevent them making plans.

Having raised three children to the age of criminal responsibility, I'm reluctant to consign the house to their care for four days running. I've seen the damage they can do while I'm here watching.

My wife has produced two pages of typed instructions that she has taped next to the fridge. Under the heading 'SHOW SOME SELF-RESPECT', it enjoins the children to maintain basic standards of hygiene. It lists edible foodstuffs and their locations, and expressly forbids gatherings of any kind. I check the document for loopholes. It's no good just telling teenage boys not to do anything stupid; you have to think of all the stupid things they could do, and ban them in writing. Then again, I think, you don't want to put ideas in their heads, because they can be tried as adults.

Our flight time obliges us to leave in the middle of the night. I bid the oldest one goodbye as *Newsnight* begins and head for bed, but when my alarm goes off four hours later, he's still up. 'Don't burn the house down,' I say, dragging our bags over the threshold.

'I won't,' he says.

'And tell the others not to as well,' I say.

The airport, barely open, is sparsely populated by zombified parents with tiny, temporarily zombified children. Once we're airside, my wife, who is a nervous flyer, insists on a large glass of wine.

'It's four-thirty a.m.,' I say.

'If I don't get a glass of wine,' she says, 'I'm not getting on the plane.'

In contrast to the rest of the airport, the pub at the far end is heaving. Nobody else is having their first drink of the day at 4.30 a.m.; most people seem to be enjoying the last of many. A few appear too far gone to board an aeroplane successfully. The atmosphere is infectious: I order a beer with the large glass of white.

'This is weird,' my wife says, looking around. 'It's too easy.'

'It's because we have no children,' I say.

'No one is fighting, or crying, or begging to be bought something,' she says.

'It's like going on a plane twenty years ago,' I say.

'What now?' my wife says, consulting her watch. 'We've got another forty minutes to kill.'

'It's your round,' I say.

Two days later, my wife is on the balcony of our hotel with her phone. The children have rebuffed all contact, even through social media, but she has ways round this.

'Uh-oh,' she says.

'What?' I say.

She turns the phone round and shows me a shaky video of the middle one attempting the Cornetto challenge against the backdrop of our kitchen cupboards. It's something I forgot to ban, but at least he isn't using my suggested point-first technique. Clearly struggling, he takes one final bite, prompting huge cheers from a large, off-camera crowd.

# CHAPTER TEN

Every adolescent cohort – organize them however you want: by region; generation; school building; social standing – will have a particular expression to denote generic incredulity. Teenagers fear credulousness; incredulity is their default reaction to everything. At that age you treat every un-corroborated statement that comes your way as if it were mind-blowingly unlikely. When people ask you things, you make it clear you can't even believe they're asking.

Adolescent conformity being what it is, a single expres-sion of incredulity usually rises up to crowd out all others. Everybody ends up using the same set of words to indicate everything from mild scepticism to shocked denial and disbelieving outrage. These days, for example, it is not uncommon to hear 'Shut up!' deployed in such a fashion by young people. Such an expression, so heavily relied upon for so many years, acquires the force of habit, so that you find yourself using it in adulthood, if only on those occasions when genuine incredulity catches you unawares.

In my adolescence that expression was 'What are you, high?'

If the person you were conversing with persisted in talking nonsense or continued to overestimate the scope of your generosity, the next step was to say, 'Now I *know* you must be high.' Often, for the sheer sake of escalation, it was permitted to skip straight to step 2:

'Hey, can I borrow your chemistry notes?'
'Now I *know* you must be high.'

That may seem a little discordant, until you understand that in this exchange the 'Are you high?' part is implied by the context: in the halls of Senator Brien McMahon High School in 1979, there was a good chance anybody you ran into was either high or extremely high. In this atmosphere the posing of a stupid or presumptuous question could be treated, for rhetorical purposes, as mere confirmation of a standing suspicion.

I should add that while the rejoinder wasn't really meant to be hostile, it could still make you unbelievably paranoid if someone said it to you when you were, in fact, wasted.

This, then, is the default expression I am saddled with, the one that still occasionally gives rise to such irresponsible exchanges as this:

'Dad, I'm going to a movie. Can I have ten pounds?'
'Ten pounds? What are you, high?'
'Plus a bit more for popcorn.'
'Now I *know* you must be high.'

This is not, I accept, a wholly appropriate response, even if I'm not actually accusing the child in question of being marijuana-impaired. While my reaction does convey the sheer extent of my incredulity (although the implication that the £10 will not be forthcoming is probably misleading), it also hints that I had a past life where I was at home among the perpetually baked. And while this is absolutely true, such an admission should have formed part of a more serious conversation with the child about drugs that I had already earmarked for the later date of never.

This conversation ends up happening well before never, on a night when my wife and I decide to drill it into the oldest one's head that no matter what moral, medical or legal arguments one might muster in favour of a more enlightened national drug policy, they will still kick you out of school if they catch you smoking pot. Our message is clear: under no circumstances are you to get caught. The boy nods, and then looks at us.

'What drugs have you done?' he says.

'Me?' my wife says. 'I've done all drugs.'

'Really?' he says.

'Well, not all drugs,' she says. 'But it would be much easier for me to list the drugs I haven't done.' I stare at her with a pointedly blank expression, as if to say: what are you, high?

'What about you?' says the boy, turning to me.

'I have done some drugs,' I say. 'But not that many. I mean, I've never taken acid, for example.'

'You've never taken acid?' says my wife.

'No,' I say.

'Nerd.'

'So is acid good?' says the boy.

'Christ no,' says my wife. 'It's horrible.'

This is not how I imagined this conversation going. I'm keen to be honest with my children about most things, but not necessarily myself. I do not like giving straight answers to questions like, 'So, are you hungover?' or 'Have you ever stolen anything?' When it comes to my biography – especially the bit from before they were born – I like to restrict the information to stories that are either instructive or amusing. If they want pathos, they can read novels.

# CHAPTER ELEVEN

Pets are meant to teach young children about empathy, responsibility and stewardship, but actually it's you as a parent who learns these things, because you're the one who ends up doing everything.

Mostly, however, you learn about death – more than you'd care to know. When our cat Lupin disappeared for three days and then turned up dead in next door's garden, stiff as a salt cod with the breeze gently lifting his fur, something inside me gave way with a lurch. From then on I maintained that we should stop getting new pets, or that we should at least stop naming them. I was overruled.

'I think Pepper is dead,' the oldest one says, peering into the hamster cage. This is a common anxiety, and not just with Pepper. 'I'm afraid the snake is probably dead,' my wife says when the snake disappears, but it always turns up again. 'I think the tortoise is dead,' the youngest says, nudging the lifeless creature with his toe, whereupon its lolling head snaps into its shell with a hiss. Pets, I am constantly reminded, are improbable survivors.

Except for Pepper. Pepper is dead. It's late and I'm not sure what to do about this, so I just close the cage, turn out the lights and go to bed.

'Pepper is dead,' I tell my wife the next morning.

She stares at me, nonplussed. I know what she is thinking. She's thinking: 'Nonsense. How could such a popular condiment become unfashionable overnight?' Finally a light goes on behind her eyes.

'I knew that was going to happen,' she says. 'Don't worry, I'll deal with it. You wouldn't know what to do.'

'What will you do?'

'I'll say I buried him,' she says, 'and then I'll put him in the bin.'

The day after that, my wife is busy killing the moth larvae that regularly migrate across the kitchen ceiling in a south-westerly direction. They're coming from one of the cupboards, even though we've cleaned them all out many times.

'You have to kill them as soon as you see them,' she says, hitting the ceiling with a broom and leaving a brown streak behind.

'I didn't know they were back,' I say.

'That's because you never take any notice of anything,' she says. I know she's angry with herself because the previous day she bought a new fish tank to replace the leaking old tank, even though I said I didn't think it leaked. She said I wouldn't notice if it broke into a million pieces. Then, just after she transferred a dozen tiny fish into the new tank, it started raining and she saw that all the water on the floor was coming from a leaking skylight above.

At lunchtime she comes into the kitchen and turns off the western I'm watching.

'You don't need telly,' she says. 'I'm here.'

She pulls out her phone and starts texting someone.

'Yes, I'm glad we've had this chance to talk,' I say.

'I'm going to Oxfordshire to look at a puppy next week,' she says, still texting.

'We already have a dog,' I say, pointing to the dog. 'Look.'

'It's one of those Jack Russells that smiles,' she says.

'I'm not looking after two dogs.'

'You barely look after one.'

'What are you talking about? I'm the only one who does anything with the dog. Ever.'

'Little smiling Jack Russell!' she says.

'We can have a new dog when the old dog dies,' I say. 'Like Pepper.'

'I'm not getting a new hamster,' she says. 'They depress me. That rubbish needs to go out, by the way. You-know-who is in there.'

'We'll always have the ceiling worms,' I say.

She scowls and stares at the fish tank. 'Now one of the fish is swimming funny,' she says. 'Christ.'

'Is it?' I say.

'You won't have noticed because you're not very observant,' she says.

'I just can't see from here,' I say, closing one eye. 'I'm out of left contact lenses.'

We both walk over to the fish tank and peer in. On first inspection, the fish seem fine to me.

'There, that little one at the back,' she says. 'He's gone a bit banana-shaped, do you see? And he's all lopsided when he swims.' He does seem to be veering to the right.

'It could be some neurological condition,' I say. 'How long would you say he's been like this?'

'Actually, I think I may have squashed him with the net,' she says.

Within minutes of arriving back home from a week away, the oldest discovers that one of his own tropical fish has perished in our absence. It's been a long journey and I'm a little short on sympathy.

'Oh, well,' I say, flipping through the post. 'Fish die.'

He goes upstairs to clean out his tank. A few minutes later I hear shouting and slamming of doors. I go up to investigate. It transpires that while he was cleaning out the tank he accidentally let one of his little fish slip down the plughole of the bathroom sink.

'That's ridiculous,' I say. 'You really need to be more careful.' Only after I say this do I realize how unhelpful it sounds, and how harsh.

I go back downstairs. Minutes later I hear more shouting and slamming. It transpires that while he was returning the fish to the tank, he let another one slip down the plughole.

'You didn't,' I say. 'What in—' I stop there. I can see he's consumed with self-reproach. It seems a bad time to tell him that life is like this, that misfortune comes in pairs, in threes, sometimes in gouts; and that it's usually all your own fault. I can tell he is thinking about the poor little fish stuck somewhere in the pipework. So am I.

'Get me a bowl,' I say. I go into the bathroom and reach behind the sink. After a brief, sweaty struggle I manage to undo the connection just beyond the U-bend, and twist the plastic pipe away from the wall.

'Here,' says the boy, entering with a bowl.

'Hold it under there,' I say. I turn on the cold tap full blast and a few seconds later water jets out of the pipe into the bowl, along with a quantity of limescale and a tiny, swimming fish.

'Whoa,' says the boy.

Now that's my kind of parenting, I think. No shouting, no swearing, no depressing life lessons; just low-level heroics, all day long.

'I wish I'd thought of that for the first fish,' I say.

'Yeah,' he says.

I can tell my family is keeping something from me. They have conversations that stop when I enter the room. They smile and hum when I ask questions. They're treating me, as usual, like a moron, only more so.

They think I don't know what's going on, but I do. I caught the youngest looking at a picture of a puppy on his phone. It appears to be the same Jack Russell my wife has on her phone, the one she went all the way to Oxfordshire to photograph.

'We do not want a dog,' I tell her. 'We have a dog.'

'Who said anything about a dog?' my wife says. 'Anyway, it's none of your concern.'

'What isn't?'

'Nothing,' she says. Then she smiles and hums and leaves the room.

Our home is already overrun with animals. Besides the dog and the cat, we have the snake, Mr Rodgers. Then there's the other snake, Mrs Hammerstein, which we are only looking after temporarily while the owners are away, although the name they gave it implies they always meant for us to have it. We also maintain a tortoise and some fish. These are just the animals we keep on purpose; I am not including the many tiny parasites we harbour. We are presently down one hamster, but in my opinion this does not create a vacancy the size of a Jack Russell. But my opinion counts for nothing.

'The absolute last thing we need,' I tell my wife, 'is another dog. Why don't we just keep pigs?'

'Little black-and-white Jack Russell!' my wife says.

Later that evening, both snakes escape. I spend half an hour shifting furniture and looking under things with a torch, getting slowly furious.

'Do you see them?' my wife asks.

'I can't see anything!' I shout from the wardrobe I am trapped behind.

'Why are you so angry?'

'This house is like a zoo,' I say. 'A bad zoo. A zoo of shame.'

'Found one,' she says. 'In here.' She is holding a stereo speaker to her eye. 'How do we get it out?'

'We don't,' I say, unplugging the speaker and shoving it in the cage. I go to sit in my office for a while, thinking of many convincing arguments against getting another dog. I imagine how embarrassing it would be to walk two dogs at once. I go down to the kitchen, where the youngest one is doing his homework and my wife is talking on the phone using the especially bright voice she reserves for strangers she wishes to charm.

'Marvellous!' she says. 'We'll see you then!' She hangs up.

'What's that?' I say.

'Nothing,' she says.

'I'm not walking two dogs,' I say. 'People will think I'm a dog lover.'

'It's really for him,' my wife says, pointing to the youngest one. 'It would be his responsibility.'

'No, it wouldn't,' I say. 'It would be my responsibility.'

'Actually, it would be my responsibility because it would basically be my dog,' says the boy.

'What about that dog?' I say, pointing to the dog. 'We could make that dog your dog.'

He starts humming and leaves the room.

'We can't get another dog,' I say. 'It's a terrible idea for many, many reasons.' I list a few, but feel as if I'm speaking in green ink. My wife no longer appears to be listening. 'So to sum up,' I say, 'there will be no dog.'

'Fine,' she says.

'What do you mean, "fine"?'

She starts humming, but I don't need an answer. I know what 'fine' means. 'Fine' means she has already got the dog.

The day is at an end and I feel drained of life. It could be because the red wine I ordered off the internet doesn't agree with me. Or it could be because my children are not in bed even though I have sent them to bed with strict instructions that they must actually go to bed. I can hear the football bouncing off the walls upstairs. I press myself to a second glass of wine – I have a whole case of it to get through – and lie back on the sofa to watch the TV flicker.

'They're playing football,' says my wife.

'I know, but I can't face the stairs,' I say. 'Maybe I'm not getting enough sunlight.' Above I hear running footsteps, shrieking and a slamming door.

TIM DOWLING

'Will you shout at them?' says my wife. I open my mouth to shout, even though I know I'm too tired to make myself heard. From upstairs I hear howling laughter which is, I notice, from this distance almost indistinguishable from distress. As I mentally log this observation for future use, it becomes clear what I am hearing is actually pure, undiluted panic. The noise is coming from all three children. My wife and I run up the stairs.

The middle one, it transpires, walked into his room to find the cat inside the snake tank; a small woodshaving had got lodged in the groove in which the door runs, leaving a gap big enough for the cat to insert a single claw and tug. By the time I get there the cat has been removed, but Mrs Hammerstein is lying lifeless on the floor of the tank with her mouth hanging open and her neck bent at an unnatural angle. Her long red body is dotted with puncture wounds.

'That can't be good,' I say. I look at the youngest one, who is horrified. The middle one is beside himself. The oldest one turns and leaves the room.

'Oh dear,' says my wife.

Mrs Hammerstein isn't even our snake. Our snake is safely tucked into the back of his favourite tin can.

'Mr Rodgers is fine,' I say. 'But Mrs Hammerstein ...' I don't finish the thought, which is that we might as well let the cat have her now. What are we going to tell the owners? They entrusted us with a healthy snake, and now we're going to give them back a belt. A damaged belt.

'Oh dear,' says my wife, again. I reach out to stroke Mrs Hammerstein but it turns out that I am no more comfortable touching a dead snake than a live one; I end up giving her a reluctant, unseemly poke. The neck unkinks, the mouth shuts, and she slowly begins to curl round herself.

'It's moving,' I say. The oldest one comes back into the room.

'This happened to a guy online,' he says. 'If they get bitten they shed their skin straight away, apparently.'

'You mean it's fine?' I say.

'There's a danger of infection, so it needs to go in a separate cage on some paper towel. And everyone on the snake forum criticized the guy for not having a proper lock.'

'It doesn't look fine,' I say. 'It's just staring madly, without blinking. Do snakes blink?'

'Go and get some paper towels,' says my wife to the middle one.

'Are we saying this snake is fine?'

The next day, on the vet's orders, we give Mrs Hammerstein a bath in an iodine solution. She is, it must be said, some way off fine – she lacks verve and seems to suffer from a curious inability to turn right – but if you'd told me the day before that I would be suffused with a renewed sense of optimism and energy just because someone else's snake wasn't dead, I'd have mumbled incoherently, poured myself a third glass of red wine and changed the channel.

A fortnight later Mrs Hammerstein remains alive, if not exactly well. The vet said there was a problem with the snake's jaw – it was either swollen or dislocated, or possibly both – and there was a bit of a kink in her neck, although I accept that 'neck' is an imprecise term when you're talking about a snake.

Against all my instincts, I take to monitoring the snake closely, opening its cage once a day and poking it to see if it moves. It's hard to tell the difference between a snake that's getting better and a snake that's going downhill, but you only have to look at its companion snake, Mr Rodgers, to see that Mrs Hammerstein remains some way off fine. From time to time I consult the middle one, in whose room the snake tank sits: 'Is Mrs Hammerstein, you know, improving at all?' I say.

'Yeah, I think so,' he says. 'She's moving more, um, realistically.'

'Does she eat?'

'Nope.'

We put the snake in the bath every few days, as a precaution. We have no idea whether it's drinking its water – no one has the patience to try to catch it in the act – and an occasional swim is supposed to help it stay hydrated. But it goes four weeks, then five, without eating anything. It's lethargic, and its bright-red colour has dulled. To me, the ultimate prognosis seems obvious. My wife takes it to the vet again, half hoping to be offered a dignified way out. Instead, she gets a lecture on the general resilience of snakes. If Mrs Hammerstein is to die, it will be on her own timetable.

A week later, I can bear no more. I want to once again be the kind of father who recovers pets from pipework; not the kind who says, 'Oh well. Fish die.' I go off in search of the middle one.

'It is time for this snake to eat,' I tell him. 'Fetch me a dead mouse and some tweezers.' I carry the snake to the bath. We dangle the mouse in a variety of ways, to no avail. Mrs Hammerstein doesn't seem to see the mouse if it is introduced from the left, so we try the right. She strikes a few times, but ends up biting her own body, which I find disturbing. When she does briefly clamp on to the mouse, it's clear she can't open her jaws far enough to get hold of it properly. It's too big.

'Maybe half a mouse,' says the middle one.

'Guess whose job that is,' I say. He goes to the kitchen and returns with a neatly scissored mouse torso. I pick up the bite-sized chunk of gore with the tweezers. We take turns for another half-hour, without success. Mrs Hammerstein is clearly exhausted, and the boy is distressed.

'This is incredibly frustrating,' I say, feeling myself un-accountably on the verge of tears. 'Poor Mrs Hammerstein.' At that moment my wife walks into the bathroom.

'What's going on?' she says.

'Mrs Hammerstein still won't eat,' says the boy.

'She seems to lack the motor coordination necessary to take prey,' I say. 'Frankly, I don't see how we're ever—'

'Oh for Christ's sake,' my wife says. She picks up the snake, pries open its jaws with a finger, takes the half-mouse off the end of the tweezers and pokes it down its throat. Then she pinches its mouth closed, massages the mouse down past the kink and hands Mrs Hammerstein back to the boy.

'Hang up that towel,' she says on her way out.

A large pull-out quote from the pages of an open magazine snags my eye. 'Animal hoarding is now a recognized psycho-logical condition,' it says, alongside a picture of two dozen cats living in a crawl space. How ridiculous, I think. Then I look around the kitchen and think: if you don't have the condition, mate, you're certainly suffering from the symptoms.

To say that the new dog is settling in well would be to imply that it has had to adjust to our routine in some way, which is not the case. Despite its having a cage all its own to sleep in, I still wake up most mornings to find that I am wearing it like a hat. In the first two weeks I could still walk into a room and think, 'A turd? On the new carpet? How incongruous', but these days this regular occurrence is just a grim reminder of our lack of progress in that department. The new dog does what it likes, where it likes.

The old dog maintained a pained denial for the best part of two weeks, steadfastly ignoring the little animal that yapped in her face and hung by its teeth from her ears. Recently, however, they have started to get on, which is to say that they play-fight for hours at a time, rolling from room to room, snarling, growling, barking and clacking their claws on the wooden floors in a desperate bid for traction. It is impossible to read a newspaper while this is going on, but it's also quite hard to watch. Every once in a while I look up to see that the little dog's head has disappeared inside the big dog's mouth.

'Don't do that,' I say. 'It will end badly.' But they do not listen. If the little dog is troubled by being partially eaten, it does not show it.

I don't like walking two dogs. I know how pro-dog it must look, and I sense vague disapproval from a certain sector of the community that regards multiple ownership as a sign of wrongheaded enthusiasm, if not a recognized psychological condition.

I also find it difficult to accept a compliment on behalf of something cute; I would much rather apologize for something ugly. I have, for example, no suitable answer to the question, 'Isn't it darling?', which, though rhetorical, still seems to demand some response.

'What's it like having two?' asks a woman with a Labrador.

'Well, it's, you know,' I say. 'It's just awful.'

'Yes, I was thinking of getting another one, but I ...' She stops and draws in breath sharply as the little dog rears up on its hind legs at her feet.

'Oh! Isn't it darling?'

'Hmm,' I say.

My wife arrives home in the early afternoon. I hear the little dog yapping in the hall, pausing only briefly, I imagine, to turn a back flip.

'What's this?' my wife says, in her squealy dog voice. 'What's this on the floor?'

It's a turd, I think. Another turd.

'Have you walked the dogs?' she shouts to me, suddenly dropping her voice an octave, if not two.

'Not since this morning,' I say.

'Shall we walk them together?'

It's just preferable, I suppose. This way, nobody need know that the cute little dog is mine, or indeed that the woman striding ahead of me and being uncharacteristically exuberant about the outdoor life is my wife. And when we are stopped halfway round by a woman who is walking a pug, a terrier and a whippet, my wife has a ready answer to the question, 'Isn't it darling?' It's quite a long answer, but it's better than nothing.

A few weeks later my wife is cross with me and, as is her wont, she is venting her dissatisfaction on the first person to ring her. 'He called me immoral for putting a dog turd in a garden waste bag,' she says to whomever is on the other end.

'It's made very clear on the side of the bag,' I say. 'Green waste only. No soil, no stones, no any other type of rubbish.'

'Well, exactly,' she says into the phone. 'Where am I supposed to put it?'

'The old dog,' I say, 'was never allowed to shit in the garden, much less in my luggage.'

The old dog raises one eyebrow, then the other, in the fond hope that I might be saying something about food in a bowl. The new dog gnaws on the old dog's leg.

'You know what he's like,' my wife says. 'He's afraid of authority.'

To be honest, I'd be ecstatic if the new dog could be compelled to perform its toilet at the bottom of the garden. This time around, the whole house-training regime has been haphazard, ineffective and punctuated by alarming setbacks. It has been ten weeks, but we are still a long way off any sort of graduation ceremony.

I am, I accept, part of the problem. Because my argument against getting the new dog went unheeded – indeed un-acknowledged – I have refused to play any part in its educa-tion. For the first few weeks I was content merely to indicate to others the location of the latest puddle of pee. After a while, I couldn't be bothered even to do that. If it was in my way, I cleaned it up; if it wasn't, I left it. I weighed the effort of maintaining a grudge against the inconvenience of stepping on the occasional tiny turd, and decided that, for the moment, it was worth it. I learned to check inside my shoes before I put them on.

My wife will say there has been some improvement, but she is being optimistic. Occasionally I hear her trying to discipline the puppy, but you don't have to be in the same room to know that the dog is refusing to make any connection between the note of disapproval in the scary lady's voice and the tidy heap of faeces on the landing.

The next afternoon I come down to the kitchen to find another pool of pee on the floor. The sun is shining, the back door is wide open and the little dog is sitting in the garden. I think it now comes inside specifically to pee.

My wife enters the kitchen.

'Some pee there,' I say, pointing. She sighs. The little dog comes in from the garden.

'What is this?' my wife says to the dog. 'What is this?'

'I think that dog is defective,' I say. 'You should take it back.'

'She's learning,' my wife says.

'Wrong,' I say. 'It learns nothing. It's completely untrainable.' My wife extends one arm and snaps her fingers. The little dog begins to walk around the room on its hind legs.

The next day is a Sunday, and I rise late. There is no pee on the landing, no turd behind the front door. My wife is already out walking both dogs.

For the first time in a long time, the house seems a quiet, civilized, vaguely hygienic place. The oldest one is sitting at the kitchen table eating breakfast and reading the paper, and I decide I will join him. I get a bowl out of the cupboard. As I walk over to the table I step in something that crackles unpleasantly as my bare foot sinks into it. I shudder as I lift my leg, letting the foot dangle in mid-air. The oldest one slouches and leans sideways to look under the table.

'Did you just step in that pile of Rice Krispies?' he asks. 'Worst feeling ever.'

In the park I meet a neighbour I haven't seen in a while. Her dog is sitting on the path, refusing to complete the journey to the shop. My two dogs are wheeling in tight circles ahead of me, growling and nipping at each other. The woman gives me a sympathetic smile.

'How's the bonding going?' she asks.

'Oh, you know,' I say. 'They get on, most of the time.'

'No, I meant you and the little one,' she says.

'It likes me,' I say, 'but I don't like it back.'

'You'll have to bond with it somehow, for everyone's sake.'

'Really?' I say.

We've had the new dog for six months, and I still have fantasies about giving it away. It smells. It chews things. Last week, it gnawed an enormous gouge into the sitting room floor trying to get at a peanut wedged between two floorboards. My wife is devoted to the new dog, but she is not home with it all day.

After we return from the park, it spends the rest of the morning haring up and down the stairs. Then it skids into my office, climbs onto the back of the sofa, presses its nose against the window and growls. This goes on for fifteen minutes until I stand up and look.

'Are you growling at that man?' I say. The man in question is smoking a cigarette in an adjacent street, about 200 yards away. The dog looks at me, looks at the man, and growls.

'He's entitled to stand there,' I say. 'In any case, it's none of your concern.'

I sit down and return to my work. The growling continues, rising occasionally to a stifled yap, presumably because the man in the street has looked at his watch. I think back to a time when the only distraction I had to cope with was the knowledge that the old dog was sitting behind me staring at the back of my head. These days the old dog spends a lot of time downstairs. The little dog growls at the man again, then yaps.

'Quiet!' I shout. This gives it a jump, causing it to slip and fall down the back of the sofa. There is a horrible muffled scratching as it tries to claw its way back up.

'I can't work like this,' I say, standing and walking out of the room. The dog is at my heels before I'm halfway down the stairs. On the landing we meet the cat, which arches its back and makes a noise like a distant air-raid siren. The dog sits down, looks at me and whines.

'Don't try to involve me,' I say, continuing down the stairs.

By the afternoon the little dog has calmed down; it pads inoffensively around my office as I write. I think about what my friend in the park said about bonding. Maybe if I made more of an effort, it wouldn't be so difficult to live with. It might even stop shitting in my luggage.

The front door opens. The little dog's ears stand up. I look down to see that it has just finished chewing the cover off my dictionary.

'Idiot!' I shout. 'Out!' It runs off. A moment later my wife walks in with the dog trotting behind her.

'What's happened?' she says.

'That dog,' I say, mustering all the icy indignation available to me, 'has just eaten my dictionary.'

My wife stares at me. 'It's not your dictionary,' she says.

'Fine. *Our* dictionary,' I say. 'The point is—'

'Did you leave it on the floor?' she says. She's trying to make this my fault, I think.

'The dog doesn't own the floor,' I say quietly.

When I go down to the kitchen at the end of my working week, my wife says I have to do something about the youngest one.

'He comes home every day and goes straight to the television … He's become institutionalized.'

I shrug, because it seems to me that when you run an institution, the institutionalization of the inmates is a desirable outcome, if not the whole point.

'Good to see he's settling into a pattern,' I say.

Meanwhile, our most recent intake, the little dog, still refuses to knuckle under, conducting itself in a manner that runs counter to all stated regulations. In violation of my express wishes, it spends all day either barking downstairs or sitting on my lap pretending to be interested in the internet. The former is, I suppose, preferable to the latter, but I can't accept that these are the only choices.

Over the last year, I have been able to divine the meaning of most of the dog's vocalizations, and our exchanges now take the form of arguments shouted from one end of the house to the other.

Dog: Someone is walking by the window!

Me: Shut up! I'm working!

Dog: Letters are coming through the hole in the door!

Me: That happens every day! Get used to it!

Dog: Someone else is walking by the window!

Me: I don't care!

One particular bark, which has a telltale plaintive squeak to it, features more and more frequently. It can be roughly translated as 'Help! I'm trapped on the other side of the cat!'

The little dog and the cat have never managed to achieve the uneasy detente that exists between the old dog and the cat, partly because the little dog and the cat are the same size, and partly because the cat has concluded – justifiably, in my opinion – that the little dog is an idiot. In all their past confrontations, the dog has come off worse, and now if the cat decides it wants to sit halfway up the stairs, it creates an obstacle the little dog cannot get round. Initially, these standoffs were an occasional accident of timing, but recently the cat has begun to do it deliberately, for sport.

Apart from the barking, the arrangement suits me fine.

Dog: Help! I'm trapped on the other side of the cat!

Me: Good! I'm glad!

Dog: Help! I'm trapped on the other side of the cat!

Me: Perfect. As far as I'm concerned, you can stay that side for ever.

Dog: What?

Me: I said, as far as I'm concerned—

Dog: Help! I'm trapped on the other side of the cat!

My wife is not interested in hearing any of this. She seems to feel that the alleged institutionalization of the youngest one is a priority.

'You're his father,' she says. 'Go and talk to him.'

'And say what?'

'Find out if he has any homework, then ask about his likes and dislikes and report back.'

I go into the sitting room. Minutes later, I'm back in the kitchen. 'He says he did his homework already.'

'Bollocks,' my wife says.

'And among his likes, he listed watching TV and me going away.'

'That's simply not good enough,' she says. 'Get back in there.'

'He's keeping his head down, doing his time, that's the main thing.'

I hear the little dog barking again. 'Help!' it says. 'I'm trapped on the other side of the cat!'

'Will you go and move the cat?' my wife says.

'I can't carry on like this,' I say.

The next morning, I wake to find the cat and the little dog sitting on either side of my chest and staring down at me. I close my eyes slowly, wondering what kind of unholy deal they've struck in the night.

My wife has been away for a week, and is returning in two days' time. It is important to me that she finds nothing negative to say about my seven days in charge; consequently I am trying to figure out how quickly I can purchase a telly identical to the one smashed in her absence, when I notice that the small dog is malfunctioning.

'What's wrong with this dog?' I say.

'It's stupid,' the oldest one says.

'It's all red on the underside,' I say. 'And it's chewing itself. What have you done to it?'

'Nothing. It was fine yesterday.'

There is no time to purchase an identical dog before my wife returns home. The oldest one and I bathe it in medicated dog shampoo. I wrap it in a towel and lay it on the bed, where it stares at me balefully. It is still staring at me when I wake up the next morning.

By the afternoon the skin condition is slightly improved, but the little dog is lethargic and downbeat. It is not interested in the early-evening trip to the park; it just sits on the grass, staring at the ground, while the big dog mingles with the other dogs. One of the other dog walkers approaches us.

'That one's not very well,' I say, pointing. The woman addresses the dog directly.

'Are you not very well?' she says. 'Oh dear! What's wrong?' The dog stares at the ground.

'It's like a skin thing,' I say. 'Probably an allergy.'

'It could be from stress,' she says. 'Have you not taken her to the vet?'

'I was going to, but they'll be closed now.' I explain that I am busy, and that my wife is away.

'Well, that'll be it,' she says. 'She's probably just stressed from being left alone with you.' This had not occurred to me.

'But I'm fun to be with,' I say. The woman looks at me for a moment.

'I don't think you're supposed to say that sort of thing about yourself,' she says.

The oldest one leaves to spend the night with a friend. I sit with the dog in my arms, contemplating the possibility that my company is stressful enough to drive an animal to self-harm. The dog stares up at me.

'We've had some good times,' I say. 'Haven't we?'

It is my plan to take the dog to the vet first thing, but I find it sleeping. It cannot harm itself while it's unconscious, I think. I decide to make a start on work and reassess at lunchtime, but I end up working straight through lunch. The dog comes up to my office in the afternoon and chews itself furiously. Fur floats on the air.

'Stop!' I say. 'We'll go to the vet in half an hour, just—' My phone pings.

It is a text from my wife that says, 'Back at 4.' It is, I notice, half past three.

'What have you done to her?' shouts my wife on first seeing the little dog. 'She's chewed all the hair off her tail!'

'That's new,' I say. 'The tail was fine this morning.'

'Right,' she says, scooping the dog into her arms. 'I'm taking her to the vet.'

When she returns half an hour later, the dog is wearing a plastic cone on its head.

'The vet is shocked by your neglect,' she says. 'She had to have an injection.'

'An injection for what?'

'Allergies. Honestly, I've only been gone a week.'

'So it's nothing to do with me,' I say. 'I am fun to be with.'

## Lessons in primatology 3

It doesn't happen very often, but it happens: my wife has for some reason taken against something I have written. I'm afraid I cannot explain the situation more fully without first taking steps to disguise the identity of some of the people involved. Safeguarding their privacy will not, I trust, undermine the basic truth of the story.

So, anyway, on Saturday morning I wake to discover that my life partner – you remember Sean – is already downstairs. This means I can expect a cup of coffee to be delivered to me shortly, even though making coffee on Saturdays used to be my role.

As I lie in bed waiting, I reflect on Sean's late and unlikely conversion to cosy domesticity. In recent months – ever since he gave up his part-time job at the behavioural primatology lab – Sean has taken up embroidery and begun producing large quantities of preserves. While it is possible that Sean's domestic phase may be symptomatic of a personal crisis that will need to be addressed in the long term, in the short term I could do with a coffee. Eventually I tire of waiting and get out of bed. I am lying in a deep bath when Sean finally appears. He does not, I notice, have a mug in his hand.

'You don't know it,' he says in a cold, hollow voice I've heard perhaps only three times in all the years we've been gay-married, 'but you just fucked up very badly.' He turns and walks out. I suffer two immediate and competing reactions: the first is a profound fear, the second a strong sense of blamelessness. I have, after all, been asleep for the last eight hours. What could I have done?

I dress and go downstairs; Sean is looking at a copy of my most recent column. As I enter the kitchen, he reads out the offending sentence twice, the second time so angrily that the dog shakes. I realize I need to choose my next few words carefully.

'I don't see the problem,' I say.

Sean explains his distress through clenched teeth: I have summarized his landmark study on primate behaviour in a way that badly misrepresents his findings, making him a laughing stock, or something.

'It could not be worse!' he shrieks. Just then, Kurt, the youngest of our three adopted ex-research chimps, waddles into the kitchen and upends a box of cereal, leaving a pyramid-shaped pile of Shreddies on the table. He makes the sign for 'milk'.

'I'm sorry,' I say.

Kurt goes to the fridge and gets the milk himself, splashing it liberally on the pile.

'How could you not see?' Sean shouts, before declaiming the sentence one more time.

Kurt makes the sign for 'Why scream?'

'You wouldn't understand,' Sean says.

Kurt signs, 'Please, I'm eleven.' He puts his hands over his eyes and shakes his head from side to side. I take this to mean 'You don't have to hide things from me.'

'It's something Dad wrote,' Sean says. 'Read this.'

Kurt tears out the page and eats it. He makes the sign for 'whatever'.

'I rather agree,' I say.

'You're going to have to show me these things before they go out,' Sean says.

'Why?' I ask. 'It's not as if I'd written about that time you tripped over the dog and knocked yourself unconsc—'

Kurt begins a cycle of alarm screeches, banging his fists into the pile of cereal, before running from the room. I'm very fond of Kurt, but I sometimes find it hard to believe he shares 99 per cent of our DNA.

'You can clear that up,' Sean says, stalking past me. In the silence that follows, I can just hear the distinctive pant-hoot of our middle chimp, Anton, from upstairs. I think he's saying there's something wrong with the broadband connection.

# CHAPTER TWELVE

Just about the time you finally begin to feel you've mastered the rhythm of fatherhood, you notice the first signs that it's all coming to an end. Even in the midst of family life, you can feel the present leaching away. Best to ignore it, I think, until you can't any more.

Some years back a photographer came to the house, took me to the park over the road and lashed me to the trunk of a huge oak tree with my own rope. Then he handed the end of the rope to my three sons and told them to smile and pull. The result was used to illustrate some article I'd written.

I can't remember where the article appeared or what it was about, but you get the idea: I could not, even then, control my children. My wife had the photo framed and hung it in the hall, where it serves to remind me how eerily compliant I can be in the company of photographers. It also shows how long I've been pitching myself as a useless father.

If only I'd known then how bad it would get. In those days, I was actually of some service to my kids. I could tie shoelaces. I could draw a cat. Now if one them says, 'Dad, I need your help,' it's invariably because he's trying to order something on the internet and has reached the stage of the transaction where you need a credit card number.

Mostly, though, the photograph just makes me feel old. It's clear from the way the children are dressed that only the oldest was of school age, and while the older two are grinning and tugging as instructed, the youngest is staring into the lens in perfect bewilderment and appears to be using the taut rope to hold himself upright. The man tied to the tree may be sporting a theatrically world-weary expression, but his face is hardly lined and his hair is dark and thick. Despite the rope digging into the flesh of his arms, he looks comparatively untroubled.

I deliberately stop and look at this photo from time to time, to chart the progress from then to now. Through this regular monitoring, I hope to process my children's growth, my own decay and the runaway train of change incrementally, or at least in manageable chunks. I do not want the passage of time to take me by surprise. I will experience change, inevitable as it may be, on my terms.

Then one day the tree fell down. I hadn't counted on that. When I went to the park with the dog before lunch it was there; when I went out after lunch it was lying on its side, all six storeys of it, surrounded by police tape. High winds had evidently blown it over, snapping the four-foot-thick trunk at its base. When I pass the photograph in the hall later, I think: 'My ruse has failed. Time continues to pass in leaps and bounds.'

The next day I drag my youngest son away from the television to go and look at the fallen tree.

'Do you remember posing for that photograph?' I say. 'The one in the hall?'

'Nope,' he says.

'Look, it's like sponge inside,' I say, kicking the rotten stump.

'Dad, you're breaking the law,' he says, pointing to the police tape.

'It's amazing, really, that it stayed up as long as it did.'

'Can we go?'

'Yeah.' I stare at the sheared stump for a moment, then gaze out at the horizon. Then I look at the stump again.

'You know what?' I say. 'I don't think this is the tree.'

'Isn't it?' he says.

'No, I think that's the tree. Over there.' I point to another oak of similar size about thirty yards away. We stalk towards it through the tall grass.

'Or maybe that one,' he says, pointing to a third tree.

'No, this is it,' I say. 'The background lines up with the picture. I always thought it was that one, but it's definitely this one.'

'Huh,' he says. The wind gusts suddenly, and I look up into the churning mass of leaves above.

'Let's not stand here,' I say.

In spite of my efforts to process change as a predictable continuum, there were further alarming warnings that my offspring would soon cease to be children. If you're a parent you will have likely witnessed many of them: they come home with short haircuts, suddenly transformed from schoolboys into trainee policemen. They begin to swear expertly in your presence. You rise from the sofa to remonstrate with one, and find yourself eye to eye with him. Soon everything they do seems to be some kind of preparation for their eventual disappearance. They completely take over your life, children, and then one day they get up and walk off with it.

It is Tuesday morning and I can't find any clothes. I know from bitter experience how dangerous it is to wake my wife with questions about my wardrobe, but I feel I have no choice.

'Where is the white shirt I left out specifically?' I say. A muffled string of expletives emanates from under the duvet, to the effect that she has sent the oldest one off to his work experience placement in it.

'In my shirt,' I say. 'I have to go on the radio today.'

'Leave me alone,' she says. I go to the closet and put on one of the shirts I had previously considered unsuitable, even for radio. Then I go back to the bedroom.

'Where are the trousers I left with the shirt?' I say. The duvet is silent.

'You didn't,' I say. The duvet doesn't say anything.

'They were basically my only available trousers,' I say. The duvet flaps down and my wife sits up.

'They actually look better on him than they do on you,' she says. 'He's got longer legs.'

'They're mine, though, and everything else is in the machine. You knew I had to go on the radio today.'

'You can wear his jeans,' she says, 'the ones hanging up. They'll probably be a bit big for you.'

'You can't just give him my clothes to wear. I don't have enough.'

'What's the word for that thing,' she says, 'where your oldest son becomes taller and bigger than you?'

'He isn't taller than me,' I say.

'You know, when your own child begins to outstrip you in all things.'

'There isn't a word for it. It's not a recognized phenomenon.'

'Bigger, better-looking, more socially competent.'

'Where is the belt that was in the trousers?'

'I'm sure there is a word for it,' she says. 'You should write about it.'

'I can't write about things that haven't happened to me yet. Please say you didn't send him off with my belt.'

'I don't know anything about your belt,' she says, folding her arms defensively.

'I can't wear these jeans without a belt. They won't stay up.'

'Wear another belt,' she says. 'It's not my problem.'

'I don't have two belts!' I shout. 'I'm not the Duke of Windsor!'

'Stop trying to talk to me about your fucking belt,' she says, disappearing back under the duvet. I stride across the room, holding up the jeans with one hand, and pull open my sock drawer with such fury that several pairs of balled-up socks fly out of it. At the bottom of the drawer I see a curled-up belt – my emergency belt. I consider shutting the drawer for strategic reasons, but I'm running late, so I grab the belt and put it on.

'Why are you going on the radio, anyway?' my wife says from under the covers.

'To talk about marital bickering,' I say. The duvet flaps down again.

'I hope you're not going to be horrible about me,' she says. There is a pause.

'I think that's what they're expecting,' I say. 'Horrible things about you.'

'Please don't be unkind,' she says.

'It's out of my hands,' I say.

That evening I head off to meet the oldest one, fresh from his day at the office, in order to go to a concert in the park. I stand in the designated spot outside the station and wait. After a few minutes I ring him.

'I'm here,' he says. 'Where are you?'

'I'm here,' I say. 'Where are you?'

'Ah, I see you,' he says. I turn to find an enormous man bearing down on me, his long arms shooting from his sleeves.

'Hey,' he says, blotting out the sun as he approaches. He offers his customary greeting, slapping me lightly across both cheeks.

'I used to have a belt just like that,' I say.

I am accompanying the youngest one to his first day of secondary school. The school itself is brand new, and the train journey begins and ends at two recently opened stations. Everything about the morning feels freshly minted, untested and exciting, even for me.

A man in a suit approaches us on the platform.

'Excuse me,' he says, 'do you make this journey regularly?'

'No,' I say. 'This is my first day!'

It is, it transpires, his first day, too – he's just started a new job. We're all thrilled. But I realize it's also my last day. The youngest one is determined to get home on his own, and hereafter he'll be another commuter, coming back every evening with sloping shoulders and a loosened tie. After today, I think, none of my children needs me for anything, except money.

At the school gates he meets up with three friends from primary school. They form a tight circle and chat conspiratorially. I walk over and touch him on the head.

'Sure you're OK coming back on your own? Because I could—'

'Yes,' he says, dismissing me with a regal flick of his hand. As I stand on the platform waiting for the 8.54 to take me home, the sky turns heavy. I am bereft.

That afternoon, at about the time we're expecting the youngest one to turn up, he rings.

'Where are you?' my wife asks him. There is a long pause, and then she says, 'Are the police with you now?'

When I meet him off the train, he is wearing an oversize tracksuit and carrying his uniform in a bag. He tells me what happened: after school, he walked with his friend to a bus stop to see him off, only to turn round and realize he had no idea where he was in relation to his rehearsed route to the train station. At that moment, a tremendous downpour began and, after several attempts to retrace his steps, he found himself lost and soaking wet in an unfamiliar part of London. He asked someone for directions and was, he insists, within sight of his goal when the policeman picked him up and took him back to school.

'That's awful,' I say, trying to conceal how oddly reassuring I find his misfortune.

'Make sure Mum doesn't tell anyone about this,' he says.

'I will,' I say. 'I can write about it, though, can't I?'

'No,' he says. 'Of course not.'

'Really?'

That night I go to a party where I meet another column-ist. She wants to commiserate. She admits she is beginning to resent her weekly obligation to turn her life into copy, to reveal bits of herself to the public, to compromise her rela-tionships by writing about friends and family. I attempt to drain the contents of my wine glass, but it's already empty.

'Yeah,' I say, shrugging. 'I'm mostly fine with all that. I just worry that not enough happens to me.' She gives me a blank look that is at once uncomprehending and withering.

The next afternoon, the youngest one makes it home without incident. I find him watching television.

'Hey,' I say, sitting down. 'How was it?'

'Good,' he says. He cranes his neck round me at the screen.

'What if,' I say, 'I were to write about what happened yesterday in such a way that it couldn't possibly upset you? Obviously I would let you read it first, and …' I pause to take a breath, wondering if I can possibly expose my youngest son to the framework of shabby moral compromises that under-pins my inner life and still get the answer I want. I don't think it's the kind of issue I can fix with a simple payment of £5. He's too old for that now. I take another breath.

'And I'd also give you ten quid to make it worth your while,' I say.

He stares at me, narrowing his hard blue eyes. 'Make it fifteen and you've got a deal,' he says.

'Nobody taught me to shave,' I say to my wife. 'I picked it up on the streets.'

'This isn't about you,' she says. I just shrug, because I think it is a little bit about me, but I know better than to say so. I avoid the subject of the oldest one's first shaving lesson for the next few days.

I'm not shying away from this particular rite of passage for complex emotional reasons. The truth is, I've never been very good at shaving. I cut myself a lot. Although largely self-taught, over the years I have actually had a few shaving lessons from hairdressers, for articles. I found the professional advice confusing, contradictory and heavily weighted in favour of certain proprietary products that happened to be sold in the establishment. To me, shaving is a question of luck: you try your best, and more often than not it doesn't work out. Like life.

Also, I have a beard at the moment, the product of eight weeks of not shaving. I didn't grow it on purpose, exactly, but I'm still pleased with it. I have found the point where sloth meets affectation, and I like it there.

On Saturday my wife comes back from the supermarket with a new razor for the boy. 'He's upstairs,' she says, 'waiting for you to teach him to shave.'

'He's still asleep, actually.'

'Well, wake him up.'

'Will I have to shave off my beard to teach him, do you think?' I say.

'Yes!' the middle one shouts from the other room. I stroke my chin. I feel as if I've just finished writing a complex equation that covers the entire chalkboard, and now someone wants me to erase it in order to show them how to spell 'CAT'.

It is nearly midday when I get the oldest one out of bed and in front of the bathroom mirror. He is irritable, uninterested and semi-conscious. Perfect, I think: we're halfway there.

'First,' I say, 'we fill the sink. The water must be very hot.'

'Why must the water be hot?' he asks.

'Good question,' I say. 'Questions will be taken at the end. Next, we splash our faces liberally, like so.'

'Getting water all over the mirror,' says my wife, who, it transpires, has installed herself in a chair behind us, her embroidery on her lap.

'Why is she here?' the boy asks.

'You think this is embarrassing?' she says. 'Try being taught how to put a tampon in.'

'That's unhelpful,' I say.

'Please go away,' the boy says.

'I'm just here for kicks,' she says.

'Then we take our razor,' I say, holding up my own razor, 'and apply the blade side to the face, using a downward motion.' I demonstrate with the razor hovering over my cheek. He watches, and imitates.

'How hard do you press?' he says.

'Not that hard,' I say. 'Let the weight of the razor sort of …' I demonstrate the optimum pressure. When I look back in the mirror, I notice I have shaved a rectangular chunk out of my beard.

'Uh-oh,' I say. 'Let me just …' I shave a corresponding slot on the other side, but it doesn't match. Before I know it, half my beard is gone. I have no option but to finish the job.

'What next?' the boy asks.

'Nothing,' I say. 'You're done. You can apply one of the many proprietary aftershave products I've been obliged to purchase over the years, but if I were you I'd just pat my face dry with a hand towel.'

'And then fold and replace the towel on the rail,' my wife says. 'Or, like your father, you could just throw it on the floor.'

'Your choice,' I say, cutting the end of my chin.

The youngest one wants me to drive him somewhere – a last-minute, Sunday evening arrangement. Normally I would refuse – in fact, I do at first – but there is something weirdly serious in his bearing.

The story he tells involves a troubled friend, some kind of dramatic run-in with parents, and a hastily arranged meeting of mates to confer. I don't really get it, but I recall a few similar incidents from my own school years, and what I felt then is perfectly reflected in his face now: I must, however reluctantly, fulfil the obligations of being an adolescent. I suspect that if he were to ask his mother to drive him to a strange park at dusk on a school night to get involved in someone else's melodrama, she would cloud up and rain all over his plan.

'Yeah, OK,' I say, levering myself off the sofa. 'But if we're going we'd better go now.'

'Thanks, Dad,' he says.

'You know where we're going?' I say.

'Yeah,' he says. 'It's right near school.'

School, unfortunately, is not very near home, and slightly off my patch. Once we reach a particular point, I am obliged to let him play navigator to my pilot, a partnership that has led to some stunningly unsuccessful excursions in the past.

'I'm coming to an intersection,' I say. 'I need a decision from you.'

'Go left,' he says.

'I can't go left,' I say.

'Sorry, I meant right anyway.'

By the time we reach the park, the sun has long since set. The surrounding neighbourhood seems at once posher and rougher than ours, but I don't know anything about it. I do not, however, like the look of the park. The silhouetted groups gathered round park benches seem posed in attitudes of menace.

'Are you sure they're even here?' I say, peering into the gloom.

'I'll ring them,' he says, swiping his phone with a finger. I begin to wish I hadn't given this outing my imprimatur by agreeing to drive. What I should have said was: ask your mother.

'If they don't answer,' I say, 'I think we should probably head—'

'Where are you guys?' he says, into his phone. 'Tesco?'

'Tesco?' I say. 'What Tesco?'

'No, up by the basketball courts,' he says. 'Which entrance?' He opens the passenger door and stands up, looking over the car towards the park's farthest corner.

'So where are they?' I say.

'OK, yeah,' he says. 'I'm just heading your way right—'

The door slams. I realize that he has, in fact, set off.

I watch as he walks along the curved path, passing one silhouetted group after another, still gabbling away. I would very much like him to put his phone back in his pocket. I keep watching until he becomes almost indistinguishable, a dark blot interrupting the playground railings. As he reappears in a pool of lamp light, a much larger figure in a white hooded top looms up, heading in the opposite direction. At the point where they meet, the hooded figure stops, pauses for a beat, then turns and follows him, barely a step behind. Then they both round a corner and vanish behind the trunk of a tree.

I suddenly find myself out of the car and running. Two women sitting on the bench near the entrance turn their heads as I pass, because I am not running with a jogger's gait, but like someone who is very late for something urgent. Once I am past them, I run even faster.

When I reach the tree, I find nothing. I spin round twice, scanning the horizon, but I appear to be completely alone. Finally I see two figures walking away from me, sharply outlined against the lights of the shops on the main road. One, gesticulating in the manner of a standup comic driven to distraction by one of life's small absurdities, is unmistakably my son. The other is the person in the white hooded top, clearly the friend he was going to meet, a head and a half taller.

I take the long way round the playground so I don't have to pass the women on the bench again. When I get back to the car, I sit behind the wheel for a while, quietly contemplating my shaking hands.

My wife likes to be involved in the lives of her children. I sometimes fear she is in too deep, but this is something I have learned from experience I shouldn't say. I occasionally feel I ought to encourage her to emulate my more hands-off approach, but I don't know how. The main problem with using a hands-off approach as an exemplar is that in practice it doesn't look like anything.

Having spent an entire morning asking earnest questions while impersonating a sixth-former in an online student forum, my wife now wants to spend lunch talking about UCAS.

'A lot of people haven't had any offers yet,' she says. 'I said I already had one.'

'Wait,' the oldest says. 'Are you pretending to be me?'

'No, I have my own login details now,' she says. 'Anyway, it's starting to get emotional. We're all very disapproving of one boy for being so cocky.'

'How do you know he isn't his own mother pretending to be him?' the oldest says.

'I think it's safe to assume,' I say, 'that the entire forum is made up of mothers pretending to be their children.'

'I only ever went on there once, to find out a test answer,' the boy says.

'They're all a bit cagey about test answers, aren't they?' my wife says.

'You need to stop,' he says.

My wife turns her attention to the middle one, who has only just risen after coming home late from a party.

'Who was there?' she asks him. 'What was it like?'

'It was OK,' he says.

'Not good enough,' she says. 'What was the worst thing that happened?'

The middle one turns to the oldest one. 'And how was your party?' he asks.

My wife poses questions that betray her unwholesome knowledge of the boys' Facebook accounts, rattling off names and incidents I recognize from my own unwholesome knowledge.

'If nothing else, this will teach you to log out after each session,' I say to them. My wife's continued probing meets with a deepening, unamused silence. I start to eat faster. There is a long, highly charged pause in the conversation.

'So,' she says finally, 'was it a kissing party?'

'Oh my God!' shouts the middle one, dropping his fork. 'What is wrong with you? Why are you like this?'

Amid further and more pointed recriminations, lunch comes to a premature end. The middle one finds himself tasked with clearing up as a punishment. For a time, the running of water, the slamming of plates and cutlery, and periodic huffs of indignation are the only sounds in the room. After some minutes, my wife turns in her chair towards the sink.

'If at any time you're prepared to apologize for telling me to go fuck myself,' she says, 'you can go and finish watching the football.'

'Are you joking?' he shouts. 'No way! Why should I apologize to you? You're the one who ...'

He pauses to contemplate the bottom of an encrusted pan, and a smile steals across his face. 'What I mean is, I'm really very sorry,' he says, dropping the pan into the sink and running from the room. 'Bye!'

'You walked straight into that,' says the oldest one, who is rooting through the fridge for more food.

'You don't have to worry,' my wife says. 'In a week's time, you'll be eighteen and I won't be able to do that to you any more.'

'Really?' he says.

'You'll be an adult,' she says.

The boy stops to consider the notion that after a random deadline set seven days hence, his parents will be required to stop ruining his life. He looks both doubtful and a little alarmed.

By Sunday evening my wife is finding us all a bit hard to live with. The children are draped across the sofas, feet up, heads lolling, staring into phone screens. Occasionally one of them shifts his gaze to watch a bit of *Dragons' Den* through upside-down eyes. I'm sitting in what I imagine to be companionable silence, but I suspect my quiet presence is also starting to grate on my wife's nerves.

'Look at all of you,' she says.

'Shh,' the middle one says. 'We're trying to watch this.'

'Don't speak to me like that,' my wife says.

'Take these to the kitchen,' I tell the middle one, indicating an array of dirty plates, one of which is resting on my chest.

'In a minute,' he says.

'I'm sick of these children,' she says. The oldest one, slouched beside her with a laptop under his chin, snorts. 'Actually,' she adds, 'it's incredibly irritating sitting here with you playing that stupid game.'

'You're incredibly irritating,' he says, rolling his eyes.

'Why are you being so horrible?' she shrieks.

'You're the one being horrible,' he says.

'Do you hear him?' my wife says to me. I keep quiet, fearing my position will be unhelpfully neutral: I know what it is to be an exasperated parent, but I also remember what it's like to be an adolescent boy whose mother is being maddening.

When *Dragons' Den* is over, my wife shoos the children out and plucks a *Sopranos* DVD from the box set. We are slowly working our way through the saga, although she's been secretly forging ahead when I'm out.

'We've seen this one,' she says, a minute in.

'You mean, *you've* seen this one,' I say. 'Who are these people? Why are they being killed?'

'Quiet,' she says.

By this point Tony and Carmela Soprano have been separated for two, possibly three episodes. Their sixteen-year-old son, Anthony Jr, is not taking it well. His grades are suffering; his relationship with his mother is strained. In one especially poignant scene, mother and son eat supper together, alone in the family home.

'You know Ringo was not their original drummer,' Carmela says with unbearable false cheer. 'That was Pete Best.'

'Is this what's called common ground?' says Anthony Jr, rolling his eyes.

'Just trying to have a civilized conversation,' Carmela says. An awkward silence blooms on both sides of the screen. I feel I should say something lighthearted about the obvious parallels, but I don't think my wife is in a mood to find things amusing.

'Can I go to my room?' AJ says. 'I'm full.'

'Am I so horrible?' Carmela says. I glance at my wife, who is watching the screen intently.

'Get over yourself,' AJ says. I wince a little at his callousness.

'Over myself?' Carmela shouts. 'What is that supposed to—' The screen suddenly freezes. My wife is holding the remote at arm's length.

'Did you see that?' she says.

'Yes,' I say. 'I can see how—'

'Just watch,' she says, rewinding.

'Get over yourself,' AJ says again.

'Look at his salad,' my wife says. 'It's green, right?'

'Over myself?' Carmela shouts.

'Now look,' my wife says, pausing the screen again. 'It's mostly red.'

'Are you suggesting,' I say, 'that there is more radicchio in this shot, as opposed to the reverse shot?'

'Yes!' shouts my wife. 'Look.' The screen unfreezes.

'Just go,' Carmela says bitterly. 'Do me a big favour.'

'Green!' my wife says.

'If you're gonna be a martyr,' AJ says, 'obviously I'll sit here.'

'Red!' my wife says.

'No!' Carmela says. 'Go! Put your plate in the sink.'

'Green!' my wife says.

At the beginning of the New Year, after a long pause, my wife recommences her haunting of various online student forums, trying to gain insight into university places on behalf of the oldest one. It is not a form of torture in which the boy has shown much interest. I find my wife in her office, scrolling through one thread after another.

'Any news?' I say.

'People are beginning to hear,' she says.

'Really?' I say.

'Yes, but for other subjects,' she says. 'Don't try and jump on the bandwagon now.'

'I won't,' I say. 'I still think it's weird that you're pretending to be your own son.'

'I'm not pretending to be him. I have my own persona.'

The next day she is still there. She doesn't look up from the screen when I come in.

'Anything?' I ask.

'A couple of rejections,' she says. 'Nothing major.'

'Perhaps if you found a thread specifically to do with his subject ...'

'I have.'

'Then you might be able to find out when the letters go out.'

'I know when the letters go out,' she says. 'Next week.'

'So what are you doing now?' I ask. She turns to glare at me.

'These people,' she says, 'are my friends.'

Over the course of the next few days, my wife's obsessive monitoring begins to affect me.

I have trouble concentrating. At odd moments my guts twist for no reason, until I remember the reason.

On the morning of the day the letters are meant to arrive, my wife gets up at 5.45 a.m. to check her computer. Fifteen minutes later, she comes back in and throws herself on the bed.

'What's happening?' I ask.

'Nothing is happening!' she hisses. 'It's six o'clock in the fucking morning! Christ, I'm hysterical.'

Before he leaves for school, my wife secures the oldest one's permission to monitor his emails all day, even though, according to the latest information, we are not expecting an email. By 10 a.m. we are both in a state of advanced panic.

'Oh my god!' I hear my wife shriek.

I find her at her computer. 'People are getting offers,' she says. 'Apparently you can tell from the weight of the envelope.'

'You need to breathe,' I say.

'What time does the post actually come?' she says. For the first time in many months, my wife looks at me as if I might be in possession of useful information; I have been working from home for fifteen years.

'Midday?'

'Are you guessing?'

'I think it varies.'

At 12.30 p.m. the letterbox snaps. We both race to the front door in time to fight over an estate agent's leaflet. As we retreat back up the stairs panting, my wife turns to me.

'We should probably start preparing for both outcomes,' she says.

'Like, get some champagne if it's good news,' I say.

'What if it's bad news?' she says.

'I don't know,' I say. 'Gin?'

I spend twenty minutes looking out of the window in the direction I've always assumed the postman originates from. As far up as I can see, the street is deserted. Finally I go to my office to compose an overdue email. When I hit send, I find the screen has frozen. I am holding down several keys at once in an attempt to remedy the problem when the post hits the mat downstairs.

I bolt from the room, but I can already hear my wife's heels striking the hall tiles hard; she must have jumped from the landing. By the time I've turned the corner between flights, I can hear an envelope being rent in strips. And then, from directly below me, my wife lets out a bloodcurdling scream.

By the time I reach the ground floor all is quiet. My wife is in the kitchen, scrutinizing a letter. The envelope lies in shreds at her feet.

'He got in?' I say.

'Of course he got in,' she says. 'Didn't you hear me screaming?'

We stand side by side reading the letter in silence.

'It's actually quite boring,' I say, 'once you get past the first two lines.'

'Oh my God,' my wife gasps. 'It's like someone is telling me I'm pretty!' With her free hand she is texting the oldest one over and over. We are struggling to make sense of page two when her phone finally pings. It's a text from the boy.

'i'm in a lesson,' it says.

'GET OUT OF THE LESSON,' my wife writes.

Much later, when the champagne has been bought, opened and consumed, and when I have been sent to get some wine to chase it with, and when the boy has gone out with friends, I return from the shop to find my wife at the kitchen table with the letter, her phone and an open address book.

'What are you doing?' I ask.

'I'm just ringing people to tell them about my brilliant achievement,' she says.

'Remember that you still need to get an A in Further Maths,' I say.

'I know it's nothing to do with me,' she says. 'But he's mine, I raised him, so I think I deserve a bit of—' Her phone rings. She consults the screen, then puts it to her ear. 'I got in!' she shouts. 'I know! Me, me, me!'

The week of celebration that follows is, for my wife, also a kind of letting go. She resigns from the student forums she has been haunting for months, and consigns to a drawer fat files of material on the subject of higher education. As far as the oldest is concerned, there isn't much more to be done.

The following Sunday, after a long nap on the sofa, my wife wakes up in a mood to parent. Over supper, the younger two find themselves on the receiving end of her critical attention for the first time in weeks, and they're not happy about it. One is berated for writing an insufficiently gripping thank you letter. The other is given a lecture about his homework and attitude. The meal ends, not atypically, with everyone storming off, except me.

When I finish, I join my wife, who is watching television. 'They're just upset,' I say, 'because it hasn't snowed enough to close the schools.'

'I should go and talk to them,' she says.

'I'd leave it, actually.'

'That's your answer to everything,' she says. 'To do nothing.'

'The benefits of my light-touch regulation will reveal themselves over time,' I say.

'I'm going up there,' she says. She grabs the remote, hits pause and leaves the room.

I stare at a single frame, frozen in time, of a woman holding a newborn baby. I try to remember the oldest being that small, but I can't. From upstairs I can hear my wife's knuckles rapping insistently at a door.

'Let me in,' she says.

'You can't just leave me here in front of a paused programme!' I shout.

'Well, you come out, then,' my wife says. I cannot hear the boy's reply; just a long, freighted silence.

'I don't even like *Call the Midwife*!' I shout.

'Unlock this door right now,' my wife says.

'I'm going to change the channel!' I shout. 'And then you'll lose the whole show!'

'Don't you dare!' she shouts. 'Bring me up a screwdriver!'

My wife has called to say she's on her way back from a business trip to Scotland – she'll be home in a matter of hours. It seems a good time to take stock.

I find the middle one sitting at my wife's computer, typing furiously into one window while watching TV in another. The youngest one is sitting on the floor, killing people on his Xbox while barking orders into a headset. They both look about two years older than they were the last time I saw them, about twenty minutes earlier. It could be their school uniforms – with their jackets off and ties pulled loose, they look like harried office workers on a deadline.

'Is that homework?' I ask the middle one.

'Haven't got any,' he says.

'Hang on,' the youngest one says. 'I got this guy.'

'Are you lying?' I say to the middle one.

'Nooooo!' he sings.

'Go left, go left, go left!' the youngest one says. Something, or someone, explodes on his screen.

'Supper will be ready in half an hour,' I say, turning towards the door.

'See you later, shitlord,' the youngest says. It takes me a second to realize he isn't talking to me.

Downstairs in the kitchen, I pour myself a glass of wine and sit down next to the oldest one. Since he turned eighteen three days previously, I have been in a rush to reframe all my dealings with him: I can no longer issue commands based on my legal right to control his destiny. I must treat him as an adult, and converse with him on a man-to-man basis. This leaves me at a temporary loss for words.

'So,' I say finally, 'have you started gambling yet?'

'No,' he says. 'I hadn't even thought of that. I should, though, shouldn't I?'

'No comment,' I say.

An hour later, we're eating in front of the TV, watching the football. The children are also watching other screens simultaneously.

'Why are we watching this match if Chelsea are playing on the other side?' I ask.

'Because I have a bet on this match,' the oldest one says.

'So do I,' the middle one says.

My wife chooses this inopportune moment to walk in the door. 'I'm so tired,' she says. 'This house is disgusting.'

'Goal!' the middle one shouts. I'm going to miss these times, I think. I begin to suspect that the youngest one may have been referring to me when he said 'shitlord' after all.


# Lessons in primatology 4

From time to time, I receive letters from readers suggesting that my wife is either a work of fiction or secretly nice to me. Obviously she finds both allegations upsetting, and for that reason I have taken steps to disguise the identities of the people I write about. This basic safeguard will not, I hope, compromise the truth of what follows.

So anyway, my life partner Sean and I have been invited to a weekend party in the country. We'd planned to take our three adopted ex-research chimps – everyone else is bringing theirs – but there's a problem. Using a series of whimpers and pant-grunts, our oldest chimp, Heinz, has made it clear he doesn't wish to come.

'There will be lots of other chimps there,' Sean says. Heinz makes the sign for 'I'm good, thanks'. We agree to let him stay behind, because he's reached that stage where he needs to assert his independence, and he can lift a chest freezer over his head.

We pack the car full of camping equipment and bananas, and set off. When we hit traffic on the M3, Sean becomes testy. In all the years we've been gay-married, Sean has hated camping. This year, he has been made to camp twice already, in highly challenging weather conditions.

'It's going to be lovely,' I say. 'I promise.' In the rear-view mirror, I can see our youngest chimp, Kurt, repeatedly making the sign for 'Are we there yet?'

When we finally arrive, I find a flat spot to pitch our tent. I was not around to pack the tent last time, and Sean, using some form of positive-reinforcement strategy, persuaded the chimps to do it for him. As a result, the guy ropes are knotted, pegs are missing and there is chewing gum stuck to the flysheet.

'You pay peanuts, you get monkeys,' I say, to no one.

I make up the air mattress with a duvet and two pillows, hoping Sean will find the experience less of a deprivation this time. He arrives as I finish, opens the tent and snatches up the duvet. 'I've bagged us a bed in the house,' he says.

'But I've only just …' I gesture to indicate our surroundings.

Sean takes in the sylvan scene, the dramatic view, the glorious summer sunshine.

'Don't be mad,' he says.

We've known most of the other guests for years, through Sean's groundbreaking work in primatology, but because we don't see them that often, it can be hard to remember whose recent paper on ape cognition has appeared in which publication. Instead, we talk about our chimps as we watch them roll about shrieking on the grass.

'Where's your oldest?' one friend asks.

'We've left him behind,' Sean says.

'Ooh,' the friend says, 'I wouldn't trust our one on his own, not for a minute.'

Sean does not like having his expertise in adolescent chimp behaviour questioned. 'Heinz will be fine,' he says. But later he signs to me: 'Ring him.'

As the party progresses, some of the older chimps break into the cider, with predictable results. Sean grows anxious. If this is what happens under the supervision of respected primatologists, he thinks, what will be happening at home? We ring again, but it's no use. Heinz cannot work a phone.

The next morning we pack up our tent quickly. Traffic is light, and we arrive home in the early afternoon, to find Heinz hanging from his tyre, watching the cricket upside down. Sean is furious.

'Is this all you've done?' he shouts. 'All weekend?' Heinz shrugs. Sean leaves the room.

'You missed a hell of a party,' I say.

Heinz makes the sign for 'whatever'.

# CHAPTER THIRTEEN

In May, the oldest one leaves school under a cloud. 'Under a cloud' is precisely the phrase the school used on the last day of classes for the upper sixth, when they rang my wife to say he was one of a group of boys who, dressed as a giant Pac-Man and the ghosts who are alternately his pursuers and his quarry, ran through the library and several class-rooms, blasting the Pac-Man theme from hidden speakers. She recounts the call in a worried voice.

'Did you act shocked?' I ask. 'Or did you admit you knew about it?'

'I said I knew about it,' she says, turning pale. 'I didn't tell them I paid for the fucking costumes.'

We hope we are entering the final phase of our parental control-freakery, at least as far as the oldest is concerned. His A-level revision, we explain, must be a matter for him alone; only he can summon up the required commitment, we cannot want it for him. We tell him this between thirty and forty times a day, shaking him awake to deliver the message if necessary.

In the meantime the youngest one is still rehearsing his French oral presentation under duress. I've memorized a page and a half of French in the process, just as I once accidentally learned to play 'Moon River' on the violin, pursuing the middle one's grade two certificate.

I shout for the youngest one to come downstairs for his evening drill.

'You can't be serious!' he screams.

'I am deadly serious,' I say.

He appears with two crumpled sheets of paper and slumps in a chair. I take the pages from him, even though I don't really need them any more.

'How do you keep the form?' I say, pouring myself a glass of wine.

'*Pour garder la forme, je fais beaucoup de sports,*' he says with hate in his eyes.

'What is the sport that you detest?' I say.

'*Le sport je que déteste est …*'

'*Le sport que je déteste,*' I say.

'I'm not doing this with you any more,' he says.

'If the words aren't in the right order, it doesn't count as French.'

'Mum!'

On the morning before his first English exam, the oldest one will not rise to receive his lecture on personal responsibility. He cannot speak, or lift his head from the pillow.

'He has a temperature of a hundred and one,' my wife says. 'He's delirious. What do we do?'

'You get some paracetamol,' I say. 'And I will shout quotations from Mary Shelley's *Frankenstein* into his ear.'

My wife rings the GP, but the woman who answers the phone cannot be induced to share her panic. She doesn't seem to consider the boy's inability to absorb quotations from primary sources to be a genuine symptom, and anyway there are no available appointments. She tells my wife to take him to A&E.

My wife ignores the advice, puts the boy in the car, drives him to the surgery and deposits him at the front desk. An hour later she returns with a doctor's letter and a course of antibiotics. The boy, it transpires, has an upper respiratory infection.

'It's ridiculous!' my wife shouts, waving the letter. 'What if I wasn't an annoying middle-class person? What would happen then?' I shudder to think. I have long regarded my wife's peremptory manner as a kind of superpower. For a time she deployed her sharp elbows in a voluntary capacity, extracting national insurance numbers on behalf of the children of asylum seekers by being demanding and icily polite on the phone. There's no question such a talent could be dangerous in the wrong hands.

The next day, grey-faced and coughing, the boy goes to school with a doctor's letter explaining his condition – a mere precaution, to be found on his person should he expire mid-test. Three hours later he is back, flushed and perspiring, forehead on the kitchen table.

'How was it?' I say.

'It was fine, actually,' he says, opening one bloodshot eye.

'Fine?' I say.

I consider the being whom I have cast among mankind, and endowed with the power to effect purposes of horror, and think about all the *Frankenstein* quotes I can now unmemorize.

\* \* \*

We have reached the end of the heady and volatile fortnight between the oldest one's last A-level and the leaving party for the upper sixth. Had he asked me, I might have suggested that he fill the idle hours with backbreaking agricultural labour, but he didn't ask. I've barely seen or heard him. His younger brothers are still noisy, but he has learned the art of stealth.

On the day of the leavers' party, however, I hear his unmistakable footfall on the landing outside my office.

'You,' I say.

The footsteps pause, and his head comes round the door. 'Yo,' he says.

'I need to be apprised of your plans,' I say, 'so that I can strongly advise you against them.'

'OK,' he says.

'Are you, for example, planning to get arrested or anything?'

'Not *planning*,' he says.

It is not until two hours before the leavers' party that he agrees to try on the black trousers I have agreed to lend him. On his hulking frame, they become three-quarter-length shorts. He cannot do them up. His face suddenly tinges pink with alarm.

'OK,' I say, 'come with me. You'll need shoes.'

We drive to Marks & Spencer, while I hurriedly dole out all the unsolicited advice I have left.

'Can I also strongly advise against you and your friends helping yourselves to the cheap red wine left over from my birthday party that I hid in the shed?'

'Mum told us where it was,' he says.

'Two bottles are missing,' I say, 'for which you owe me a surprisingly modest amount.'

'Have you had lunch yet?'

'It's five,' I say. 'I eat lunch in my lunchbreak, at lunchtime. I strongly advise you to do the same.'

We head straight for the black trousers section of the mens' department. The boy pulls a pair off the nearest pile.

'These look OK,' he says, 'don't they?'

I examine them from several angles. 'There's nothing obviously wrong with them,' I say. 'The fitting rooms are over there.'

I point and he walks to the back of the shop, returning almost instantly with the trousers draped over one arm. 'They're fine,' he says.

'I didn't even see you in them,' I say.

'You don't need to see me in them,' he says.

We cross over to the till. Outside the shop, I hand him the bag and consult my phone.

'That took four minutes,' I say. It occurs to me that men should always shop in pairs.

'Which means you have time to buy me a sandwich,' he says.

At six o'clock, he appears downstairs, dressed and ready to go, the black of the trousers a near enough match for the jacket he's wearing.

'You look very smart,' his mother says.

'I would strongly advise you to tuck your shirt in,' I say.

'Are you sure?' he says.

'Trust me,' I say.

'I'll need a picture,' my wife says. She stands with the boy in front of the kitchen door, on the spot where he posed in his new uniform on the first day of primary school, age four. He also stood there in every Halloween and school play costume he ever wore.

Today, he is harder to squeeze into the frame. I hold my breath as I line up the shot on my wife's phone screen, experimenting with a horizontal composition before returning to the vertical to get both heads in. When I finally exhale, a shudder runs through me. My throat closes without warning. I press the button, and then blink several times to get my swimming vision to hold still.

'I'd better do another one,' I say.

I arrive home from a trip on a Sunday night in mid-July. The remains of a big lunch are spread across the kitchen table. A large box of Lego pieces, which has been dragged from a cupboard to entertain a visiting toddler, is sitting on the sofa. The oldest one and the middle one are presently using the Lego to create constructions chiefly designed to explode impressively when they collide, having been fired at one another across the sitting room floor. It's a game that used to set my teeth on edge ten years ago. Now I find it rather soothing.

The oldest one's overstuffed backpack is propped against a chair in the corner. His paperwork is neatly stacked on the table next to it. My wife looks at the backpack, and then the oldest one, and then me.

'He's going tomorrow,' she says.

'I know,' I say. She keeps looking at me, her eyes edged with insistence. It's like the expression she deploys when she's trying to remind me to tip someone.

'What?' I say finally.

'Well,' she says. 'Did you go off to Vietnam on your own when you were his age?'

'I didn't have to,' I say. 'They stopped the draft when I was ten.' I see what she's getting at: this is a big deal. I'm just not sure what she wants me to do.

There's an enormous crash at my feet; the air fills with Lego.

The middle one is sent to bed at eleven. My wife and I sit with the oldest one in the garden, reviewing a mental checklist of things he needs to purchase at the airport and repeating our warnings about the draconian drug laws in South-East Asia.

All our friends told us to make him watch *Midnight Express* before he left, but we showed him *The Deer Hunter* instead.

'It's more touristy now,' I say, 'but you get the idea.'

'How would you know?' my wife says. 'Did you go to Vietnam on your own, straight out of school?'

'No,' I say. 'I spent the summer working in an ice factory, making ice.'

'Really?' the boy says.

'You think ice makes itself? It doesn't.'

'So we're talking about you now, are we?' my wife says.

'It was back-breaking,' I say. 'I cried on my first day.'

'I'm going to bed,' my wife says, standing up. Even in the dark I can tell she's making her insistent eyes.

Alone in the garden, I pour myself and the boy a glass of wine each. I'm casting about for something significant to impart, because I'm pretty certain it's what my wife was hinting at, but I can't think of anything.

We sit in silence.

'Actually,' I say, 'the ice does sort of make itself, but some-one has to put it in bags.'

'Huh,' the boy says.

'Be sure to email,' I say. 'You have no idea what it's like for a mother to send her oldest child off to Vietnam.'

'I will,' he says.

'And don't forget to come back,' I say. 'I don't want to have to go out there and retrieve you, like at the end of *The Deer Hunter*.'

'Yeah, OK,' he says. 'I think I'm going to go to bed.'

'Me, too,' I say, stretching my arms. I go inside to lock up and turn off lights, trying – and failing – to imagine how I will feel this time tomorrow.

On my way back to the kitchen I step on something pointy in the dark, which sticks to the sole of my bare foot. I meet the boy at the garden door.

'I'll probably never have the chance to tell you this again,' I say. 'But you need to pick up all your Lego, right now.'

The next morning we take the boy to the airport where he meets his two travelling companions. It is almost unbearable to watch three boys continually drop vital documents on the floor while juggling sheaves of paperwork. I just smile and think: there is no way they're going to make it as far as the plane. But they do.

In the two weeks following his arrival in South-East Asia the oldest has offered up just a single fragment of communication – a Facebook message consisting, in its entirety, of the word 'YO'. This was to be expected – I remember being his age well enough to understand that to experience true independence from one's parents they must, at least temporarily, be dead to you – but I also knew my wife would not leave it at that.

'I've found him,' she says one morning, prodding me awake. 'He's in Laos.' It's clear that she has been up for some time, possibly all night.

What she has actually found is the blog of a twentysomething Australian IT consultant called John. John is from Bondi Beach and likes running, wine, movies and opera singing. His favourite films include *Star Wars*, *Alien* and *Whistle Down the Wind*. He has travelled extensively through South-East Asia, and it is a mere coincidence that he finds himself on the same five-day guided tour of Laos as my oldest son.

I'm not sure how my wife found the blog, but when I went looking for it later all I had to do was type the oldest one's name and 'Laos' into Google. It's a fairly exhaustive chronicle – part travelogue, part potted history, part food diary – with plenty of pictures: landscapes, temples, John sampling a glass from a clear jug of rice wine in which several bear paws are steeping. The middle section includes a long account of a boat trip up the muddy Mekong River. It's a bit like the screenplay for *Apocalypse Now*, but with more exclamation marks and the prices of all the drinks listed in Australian dollars.

My wife and I pore over each new upload with a combination of fascination and frustration. Our son is a very minor character in John's narrative. He occasionally turns up in a picture, one of twenty tourists seated round a restaurant table, or at the far left of a posed group in a cave, smiling, with a torch strapped to his forehead.

'He's changing his shirt,' I say. 'That's good.'

'Are you sure that's the back of his head?' my wife says.

He's namechecked on one or two occasions, but in the most recent entries he doesn't figure at all, unless you count oblique references to 'the rest of the group'. We know he's seen a jug of rice wine with bear paws floating in it, but we don't know if he had any.

'At least we know he's OK,' I say.

'How do we know that?' my wife says.

'Because if anything terrible happened, it would definitely be interesting enough to earn a mention from John.'

Sadly the day comes when the tour ends and the oldest one and John part company. John is off to stay with his friends Lucy and George in Bangkok, which is more than we know about our son's movements.

'I think I can hack into his email,' my wife says. 'Give me time.'

The boy rings from Vietnam two days later, catching my wife as she's getting into the car.

'How is it?' she says.

'I wish I could tell you I'm having a good time,' he says, before inserting a long, provocative pause. 'But there's a problem.'

My wife also pauses when she recounts this bit to me an hour later, because she wants me to experience something like the bolt of terror that shot through her as she sat in the car, wondering whether he was in hospital or behind bars.

'What is it?' she says, her throat closing on the words.

There is another pause.

'The bank stopped my card,' he says.

*　*　*

The day before the oldest one leaves for university, he takes to wandering absent-mindedly through the house with a glazed look and a sock in each hand. It's like watching myself freak out in a mirror, and it disturbs me to think that, among other traits, I have bequeathed the boy the mannerisms of panic.

When my wife enters the room, she fixes me with a hard stare and mouths the words 'Talk to him'. She suggests a walk in the park, and the boy goes off in search of the socks he is already holding.

In the park, I try to think of calming things to say. I tell him about my first day at college, but I cut the story short when I realize it ends with me shouting, 'What do you mean, you're leaving?' at my parents and then spending a long hour sitting alone on a bed watching dust float on the air. I decide it's better to speak of other things. I give him a brief history of the illegal dumping of tyres at the back of the park.

'They just pull up behind there,' I say, 'and dump them over the wall in the night.'

'And they roll all the way down here?' he says, kicking a tyre that lies in our path.

'Some do,' I say.

The next morning, as we put his boxes into the car, it becomes clear that he has grave reservations about the whole notion of tertiary education.

'It's going to be fine,' my wife says, 'and you can come home whenever you want.'

'No, I can't,' he says. 'You've rented my room.' Unfortunately, this is true: my wife's goddaughter is moving in almost immediately.

'That's temporary,' my wife says. 'Your room is yours when you need it.'

I ceremoniously hand over the spare key to his bike lock, which I have kept on my key chain for years. He attaches it to his keys.

'Actually,' my wife says, 'leave your house keys behind for now. I'm not sure the other two have a set between them.' She holds out a flat palm and the boy gives her a wild-eyed look.

'If you try to take these keys off me,' he says, 'I'm not going.'

As we drive out of London, my wife chatters nonstop to keep the mood light. I try to join in, but I find my voice has a deckled edge that's incompatible with amusing observations. When we pass a billboard advertising mortgages that reads 'Because a Place to Call Home MATTERS' alongside a picture of a dog, I realize I am very close to crying. I blink and roll down my window.

'Can you roll up your window,' the boy says.

On arrival, everything changes for the better. We pull up beside a white marquee, where jolly students in 'Welcome' T-shirts wait to greet us. The boy puts on the brave, smiling face of the urgently outgoing.

The car must be moved as soon as we've unloaded; the road is narrow, and there are other shellshocked parents behind us. A man in a high-visibility vest issues complex parking instructions that include two tight bends, some doubling back, a code needed to raise an automatic barrier and a warning about a fixed-penalty notice for turning left instead of right.

'You can handle that,' my wife says, tossing me the keys.

'Wait,' I say. 'You're just going to leave me here?'

My wife and son disappear into the tent. I have no choice but to get in the car and drive off into the unknown. I can't stay where I am, and I can't back up.

I sense the annual approach of the moment when my wife draws me aside and politely asks me to stop ruining Christmas. It's one of those Yuletide harbingers that seems to come earlier every year, like the one where my debit card is declined by someone wearing a Santa hat.

I would like to be able to oblige my wife, but I don't feel the matter is entirely under my control. Christmas, as far as I am concerned, is self-ruining, full of unrealistic expectations, disasters-in-waiting and panic-buying.

My wife has already selected a date for the purchase of a Christmas tree. Normally I would protest that it's far too soon, starting an argument that lasts until the tree is up and decorated that afternoon. But this year I lack the strength to protest, and it is also the day the oldest comes back from university.

Then I think: I will take my sons to buy the Christmas tree. Instead of bickering about price and size, we will laugh and grow apple-cheeked and buy a tree we'll have trouble getting into the car. It will be like all those memories I have of buying a Christmas tree with my father – many of them false – rolled together. And even if it's not the most special tree-buying expedition ever, it will look like it to strangers.

I am late for the oldest one's bus, and find him walking along the road with his bag, looking cold and hungover.

'I'm wrecked,' he says.

'We're going to buy a tree!' I say.

'Ugh,' he says. 'Take me home.'

As soon as my wife sees him, he is excused from the tree-buying expedition. No matter, I think: he'd only take up room in the car.

I go up to the middle one's room. 'Shoes on!' I say. 'We're going to buy a tree!'

'Nah,' he says.

'It's a tradition!' I say. 'A new annual tradition!'

'I'm good, thanks,' he says.

I find the youngest one where he always is – in front of the Xbox – and pull the controller from his hand.

'Get in the car,' I say.

The tree lot is very busy. There are young people in green fleeces ready to assist customers, but we keep being passed over in favour of later arrivals. Either I'm not good at looking needy, or I'm way too good at it. Instead of asserting myself I stand stupidly among the netted spruces, watching a young person who has promised to be right with me leave for lunch.

'You need to get some help,' the youngest one says.

'Yeah,' I say. 'I've heard that before.'

Finally, after exhibiting a certain amount of petulance in the cabin where the till is kept, I am assigned my own sales assistant and shown a tree.

'How tall is that?' I ask.

'That's eight feet,' says the young person. I pretend to assess its proportions while rolling one eyeball towards the sign listing prices by height. The sales assistant juts his chin expectantly. I've only seen the one tree, and already I feel as if I'm testing his patience, and the patience of my son, and of the many people waiting to be helped. I feel I am testing the patience of Christmas itself.

'Don't tell Mum what it cost,' I say as we try to jam the tree into the car.

'You're just gonna have to drive with the branches in your face,' the youngest one says.

My wife opens the front door as we're hauling the tree up the steps. 'Wow,' she says. 'It looks like your father finally got the tree he wanted.'

Slipping into the kitchen, I take another look at the receipt. I see the price includes the planting of a corresponding tree in Africa, which makes me feel a bit better. I bin the receipt and return to the sitting room, where my wife and children are holding the tree and marvelling at its height.

'There is no way that's going to fit into our stand,' I say.

'All right,' my wife says. 'Let's not ruin Christmas.'

## Lessons in primatology 5

From time to time I'm obliged to address complaints about how undignified it is to be a character in someone else's chronicle. Normally I can justify the intrusion by pointing to something I have recently paid for, and shrugging in a way that suggests an ongoing invasion of privacy is simply the price one pays for *Which?* magazine's top-rated dishwasher. Occasionally, however, it becomes necessary to blur the identities of real people. This additional precaution will not, I hope, still be fooling anyone at this point.

So anyway, my life partner Sean is bemoaning our domestic situation in his usual barbed but amusing fashion.

'This house is collapsing,' he says. 'And you do nothing.'

I point to the hanging light above the kitchen table that I rewired not three weeks ago, and flip the switch at the wall. The light comes on, and I bow slightly from the waist. Then the bulb falls out and lands in the fruit bowl.

Sean sighs heavily and pushes a card across the table for me to sign. Anton, the second-oldest of our adopted ex-research chimps, is seventeen today. It can be hard to find a suitable present for a near-adult chimpanzee, although they only ever want one of two things: new tyre swing or Nando's voucher. In any case, it's nearly midday, and Anton's still asleep.

Kurt, the younger chimp, surfaces first, bounding into the kitchen and making the sign for 'What's up?' Sean slides another card across the table and makes the sign for 'sign'. Kurt picks up a permanent marker and draws all over the card, and across much of the table.

Eventually Anton comes downstairs, blinking and yawning. 'Happy birthday,' Sean says, handing him a card. Anton shreds the envelope and eats it, before finding something inside. He examines it carefully, makes the sign for 'Nando's voucher' and turns his lips inside out.

'You're welcome,' Sean says.

In the afternoon, we all go to the cinema. Many people, including some leading primatologists, might question the wisdom of taking two ex-research chimps to see *Foxcatcher*, but it's important for them occasionally to leave their specially adapted environment. Anyway, if you put hoodies and glasses on them, most of the time no one says anything.

The trouble doesn't start until after the film, when, as we leave the cinema, Sean signs, 'What did you think of that?'

Kurt replies with two thumbs up, but it is clear from the increasing volume of Anton's cycle of distress calls that *Foxcatcher* was not his cup of tea.

'I agree that the narrative got a bit elliptical in the middle,' I say, 'but if you just allow yourself ...'

Anton embarks on a series of distinctive pant-hoots, and assumes a defensive posture, which seems to suggest that if you can't make a character's motivations apparent, you haven't got a story worth telling.

Kurt makes the sign for 'Shut the fuck up'.

Anton makes the sign for 'You shut up'.

Sean signs, 'Please don't do this here.'

Anton signs, 'Why are you blaming me?'

The argument resumes over supper, with Sean making repeated attempts to mediate. 'Stop being so aggressive!' he shouts. Anton turns an angry backflip and leaves the room. Kurt climbs onto the table and rolls in his food, before following Anton upstairs. 'Why are they like this?' Sean asks with transparent exasperation.

'The thing is, you make it worse when you intervene,' I say. 'Let them have it out.'

'You would say that,' Sean says.

'Indeed,' I say. 'I've written a respected primatology paper on the very subject.'

'Just do nothing,' Sean says, 'is your answer to everything.'

'It's a constant battle to maintain position in a linear dominance hierarchy,' I say. 'It's not really about *Foxcatcher*.'

Sean makes the sign for 'Shut up'.

# CONCLUSION

There is a large package on the kitchen table, addressed to me.

'What's in it?' my wife asks as I lift its lid.

'Socks,' I say. 'Socks in a box.'

'What for?' my wife says.

The youngest walks in. I read the note that came with the socks.

'A PR company has sent me some posh socks as a Father's Day gift,' I say. 'Also, some coffee.'

'Why you?' the youngest says.

'Because I am one of Britain's most beloved fathers,' I say.

'No, really,' he says.

'Father's Day isn't even a thing,' my wife says.

I hold up a pair of socks with a monogrammed T on them. 'I think you'll find it is,' I say.

On Sunday morning, I lie in for as long as I can, but my wife proves the more determined sleeper. Eventually I give up and get up.

'Please bring me a cup of tea,' she says, opening one eye.

'Of course,' I say. 'The perfect start to a perfect Mother's Day. Except *it's Father's Day.*'

'Nobody gives a shit about Father's Day,' she says. 'Anyway, I'm taking you to the cinema.'

'You're taking the children to the cinema, and you're making me come.'

'Fine,' she says. 'Don't come.'

I take the dogs to the park, then sit in the garden by myself. The *Archers* omnibus, blaring from two radios on different floors, echoes through the house as if it were being performed in a cathedral. After a few minutes, the dampness of the bench I'm sitting on drives me back inside. I find my wife in front of the computer, the youngest one by her side.

'*Jurassic World*, three o'clock,' my wife says. 'We can go to lunch before.'

'There won't be any tickets,' I say. 'It's the most popular movie ever. And it's Father's Day.'

'There are plenty of tickets,' my wife says.

'Happy Father's Day, father,' the youngest says in a plummy voice he normally uses to heap scorn on outmoded formalities.

'Yeah, cheers,' I say.

The oldest one, recently arrived back from university, is the last one out of the house, with wet hair and untied shoes. The last time we all piled into the car as a family, we had a different car. As my wife turns onto the ramp of a rooftop car park, I involuntarily lurch away from the passenger door.

'What's wrong with you?' she says.

'You were a bit close on my side,' I say.

'You seem to be under the impression that this car is bigger than it is,' she says. 'It's not a 4×4.'

'It is sort of a 4×4,' I say.

'No, it isn't,' she says. 'It's smaller than the old car.'

'You just don't want people to think you're a 4×4 mum,' I say.

'That's not what a 4×4 mum is,' she says.

'It has the shape of a 4×4,' I say.

'A 4×4 mum is a woman who has four children by four different fathers,' my wife says. 'I have three children, all by the same idiot.' The tyres squeak against the concrete as she pulls into a parking space.

'I think that counts as a zing, Dad,' the youngest says.

'Don't say "zing",' I say. 'Say "burn".'

In the restaurant where we have lunch, there is a card on the table advertising a Father's Day special. 'Book now,' it says. I look up: the place is almost empty. Maybe Father's Day really isn't a thing.

And, really, why should it be? What have I bequeathed my children? They're the ones who taught me how to be a father, more or less from scratch. Before the first one came along, I knew nothing. By the time he was two, I could cut a baby's fingernails without feeling faint. Over the course of twenty-odd years the three of them extracted what they needed from me; I learned all my lessons in retrospect. I only mastered fatherhood in time for it to be of no further use. That part of my life – shockingly brief, in hindsight – is almost over. But still, I think, it's nice to be here, all of us together, on a random Sunday.

'Your father is staring into space,' my wife says. 'Who's going to volunteer to talk to him?'

'I will,' the middle one says.

# ACKNOWLEDGEMENTS

Many thanks to Nick Pearson, Mark Handsley, Lottie Fyfe and Alice Herbert at Fourth Estate. Four *Guardian Weekend* editors – Melissa Denes, Clare Margetson, Sue Matthias and Merope Mills – have been obliged to put up with me across a decade and 500 columns. They've given me tremendous freedom and, when necessary, they have reined me in.

I owe a great debt to my agent Natasha Fairweather for her patience, not to mention her blind faith. This book, like the ones before it, stands as a tribute to her misplaced confidence. I am grateful to my wife for her ability to remind me – sometimes with nothing more than an arched eyebrow – that writerly hysterics butter no parsnips.

Above all I would like to thank my three sons – oldest, middle, youngest – for the grace they have always displayed about having their childhoods cobbled into subject matter. They've never complained, unless shouting 'This is all lies!' counts as complaining. I know I can never repay them, and I wish they would stop invoicing me.